CHANNELLED COMMUNICATIONS FROM SIRIUS, ARCTURUS, PLEIADES & BETELGEUSE

BERYL CHARNLEY

Copyright © Beryl Charnley

Copyright © Purple Spirit Press 2017

All rights reserved. No part of this publication may be reproduced, stored in a retrieval system, or transmitted in any form or by any means, electronic, mechanical, photocopying, recording or otherwise without the prior permission of the copyright owner.

Original transcription of the channelled work in the 1980's and 1990's by Beryl Charnley
Transcribed and typed by Gordon Charnley
Digital A5 formatted and typed in 2013 by
Heather Charnley
Second edition re-formatted in 2016 by Heather Charnley

ISBN 978-1-907042-32-4

PURPLE SPIRIT PRESS
Heather Charnley,
2 Whitesmiths Cottages, Dalston, Carlisle,
Cumbria, CA5 7QF.
Tel: (01228) 711050
Email: purplespiritpress@hotmail.co.uk
heathercharnley@googlmail.com

There are many more channelled works being issued all the time, as well as other topics.

Please contact if you wish to have more details.

CHANNELLED COMMUNICATIONS FROM SIRIUS, ARCTURUS, PLEIADES, & BETELGEUSE

SECTION ONE
SIRIUS

CHANNELLED COMMUNICATIONS FROM SIRIUS
Section One

CONTENTS   **Page**

Foreword	5
Section 1 – Oron	6
Section 2 – Oron	10
Section 3 – Oron	13
Section 4 – Oron	17
Section 5 – Oron	21
Section 6 – Oron	25
Section 7 – Oron	29
Section 8 – Oron	33
Section 9 – Oron	36
Section 10 – Oron	39
Section 11 – Oron	42
Section 12 – Oron	45

Channelled by Beryl Charnley

FOREWORD by BERYL CHARNLEY

In the early 1980's I began meditating, and not long afterwards I received channelled teachings from the I Am Presence initially, and from then on, angelic beings, in fact, Archangels Michael and Gabriel, and eventually Master Jesus (Sananda being his name now) and Master R (Rakoczi or St Germain), over a number of years.

Later, other beings contacted me from various planets, and gave me their teachings, which was interesting too, and they described themselves to me. This book encompasses the beings from Sirius, and the other three sections in the book, who are from Arcturus, Pleiades and Betelgeuse.

These various teachings will be of interest to anyone with an enquiring mind, and who wishes to expand their spirituality.

Spirituality is an important part of the journey of life for us all, a most beneficial part of it. I hope you will enjoy reading the contents of this book, and find it of interest.

Beryl Charnley

CHANNELLED COMMUNICATIONS FROM SIRIUS
ORON-1

We greet you, Beryl and Gordon, this night. There are three of us within this room to meet up with you. I know that you are aware of our size, and that this seems to be rather a small room for us to appear, nevertheless, it is possible, and we are very happy to make this historic meeting. We hope that there will be many communications successfully completed in a short while. You have been trying to reach your consciousness to a higher level, and this is good, because it makes the union of minds easier. We are obviously on a higher level than yourselves, and for this reason we feel that it is necessary to make this contact, so that we can help those who are aware of us, to pass on our knowledge and our thoughts of concern for those upon Earth. As you know, we have been watching over you for many years, and although we are not in constant contact with those upon Earth, we have from time to time sent messages, both of hope and concern for the Earth dwellers.

It has been some time since mankind began creating havoc with his planet, and we stand aside to allow him to have his free will, but as you know, there has been much pollution and change of climate as a result of man's work upon this planet, not necessarily for the good of the planet, but in creating pollution and disruption upon it. It has been noted that this has gradually built up until at times there have been dreadful occurrences, such as oil spills upon the oceans of the world, which have caused tremendous problems with fish and other creatures that live within those oceans, and bird life and innocent people have been affected upon the shores, mostly caused by thoughtlessness and carelessness. This must stop, or else there will be dire consequences. We are not predicting that the end of the world is nigh, but we are very concerned that the planet itself with its safety features will shrug off mankind in some catastrophe.

There have been some changes over the years, mainly with hurricanes, and this has caused great devastation right across, from America to Britain, and as a result, people know the changes in weather patterns throughout the globe. These are due partly to man's presence on the planet, resulting in dramatic changes. Our own planet has suffered in the past, and this was why we felt we might be able to warn mankind of what we ourselves have gone through. There have been many changes upon Sirius, in the same way, and although the features of our planet are different, the same reactions can occur as a result of the beings that live upon it, causing change that is not for the good.

Over the years, predictions have been made about the Earth, some of them quite laughable, but others are perfectly possible, some have been self-inflicted by man. Suggestions have been made that the whole of the Earth will be completely polluted, and might blow up in a nuclear holocaust. This could happen in some way, of course, if man does not take great care of nuclear activities. There has been dumping of waste within the ocean, and it must be told that in some parts of the world where power stations exist, much has been kept under cover about the possible disasters that could occur, and the illnesses through working there. At Sellafield, workers can contract leukaemia, and in fact also their families are being affected in this way. These facts should be brought to light, because there are great dangers concerned with nuclear power stations, and anyone working with these powers can be greatly affected in a number of ways.

As you know, during the Second World War, nuclear bombs caused great damage to the Earth, and everyone within the vicinity of that explosion was affected in some way. When the atom was split originally, it had not been realised that this would be used for purposes such as bombs. Those who made the discovery had not thought of the dangers concerned, and scientists thought they had discovered something to be used for the good of mankind, but sadly it has been used for bad as well as good, and over the years, many thousands of people have been affected as a result of that discovery.

Even those who thought they were working under safe conditions have found that the contrary was true. This is not just in Britain, it has occurred in other countries such as America and Russia for instance, and workers there have been badly affected.

However, I will not dwell on these sad topics, but I wish to speak of future times, when man and the Earth are uplifted to a higher vibration, and when this occurs, these changes will be brought about gradually. Slowly but surely even now, mankind and the planet are lifting up to the fourth dimension, which is the astral plane. It is a gradual process, but changes have already begun, and as has been said, gradually lifting upwards to the fourth dimension, and then to the fifth, which is even more finely tuned. It is difficult for you to visualise how it would be, but imagine your bodies becoming lighter and your need for food less. Everything will become finely tuned, and you will not have such coarse food, or the need for as many meals as you do at present, because changes will be occurring within the planet to alter the climate as well. It is well known that when you are in a warmer country, there is no necessity for food to keep you warm, and as a result, man will eat more natural foods, vegetables and fruit, and perhaps nuts and other lighter foodstuffs.

Changes will come about very gradually, but you will have less need of electric power, because warmth will not be required so much. It will also affect your daily living, and in time, there will be less industry, life will become simpler again, similar to when man first came down to Earth and lived on Lemuria. You will find that your life will become changed in many ways. As I have said, the climate will alter, and has been changing as you have noticed. The winters, generally, will not be so rigorous or so intense. You will still get pockets of cold weather, shall we say, but throughout the whole of the year there will be less change with the seasons, making it more temperate everywhere. You have noticed this, in that you have not seen so much sun in the so-called summer in this country, but I think that in future days that will change, and you will have a good summer most years, the springs and autumns will be warmer, and there will be less snow and ice. There will be less need to search for coal and oil to heat the gas turbines in industry, and less mines to excavate for coal because industry does not require this any more. It is gradually becoming less dependent upon burning coal to create transport and power.

You will find that men's lives will change in many ways. It seems a disaster at present that pits closed, and those men lost their jobs, but just think what a different life they will have. Instead of burrowing away in the darkness under the earth for most of their lives, they will be in the open in different types of occupation. Gradually there will be changes, so that men will share their jobs of work, because there are insufficient jobs for everyone, so there must be unity. Jobs can be created in this way, if men will be satisfied with working fewer hours, and sharing these jobs with other people. Something of this sort will have to happen before the latter days end. Those latter days mentioned in the Bible.

Our planet went through the same process, and we had to adapt ourselves rather similarly to this, and although Sirius has upon it a civilisation that is extremely evolved in many ways, changes were made years ago when a similar situation arose, and we had to adapt our lives into fitting in more closely with one another, as you will have to do. I think this will be accepted gradually. There are always some who cause problems, and are ready to rebel. It may seem strange to you at first, but I think that most people will eventually understand that there have to be changes in order that all can receive benefit from the jobs available. At present, there are too many people upon the Earth, and as a result of this, the jobs are scarce. All due to making life easier by creating machinery and computers that do all the work of many people, so less jobs are necessary to run the system.

You will find out that over time, when the time comes for the real changes, jobs will become less important, and survival the most important of all, the survival of those who are aware. Those who have attempted to progress and evolve, learning the Ancient Wisdom, and becoming aware of their own spirituality, and helping others develop this awareness. This will be a means of remaining upon this planet, and those who have not developed this awareness will find that in time they are left behind, literally and metaphorically. They will be swept aside, and will return to incarnate upon another planet that will be on the third dimension, as this one is presently, but you and others like you, are rising upwards as the Earth is presently doing. This time is not too far ahead. I cannot say in earthly years how long, but perhaps within the next ten years that change will be complete, and man will be a being of light, a pure being of light once more, as he was when he first evolved.

You hide your light under a bushel, but each one of you has that spark within you, and we know that it does not take much to ignite this spark to be similar to what we are, beings of light, who are attempting to help at this time. When you have reached our capabilities, we will be able to leave you, but until then, we hope that over these intervening years, we can help whoever will listen to us. Try to always meditate each day, raising your consciousness ever higher, so that you will be able to receive the highest possible communication that is waiting for you within the etheric. Each one of you is capable of linking with other beings from the higher worlds, who wish to renew your acquaintance. We have all met up before on other planets, but that is another story. So I will leave you now. My two companions and I wish you both well, and give you our blessing. Thank you for listening, and we hope to meet again next week. God bless.

CHANNELLED COMMUNICATIONS FROM SIRIUS ORON-2

Yes Beryl, we salute you both this night, and are pleased to meet up with you again. Once more we have three of us joining you in the room, we come in friendship and are concerned for your planet. We know that your friendship is given to us, and we appreciate this warmth emanating from you. We come to help humanity at this time, and we hope that we can give forth of our wisdom and capabilities for now, and future days. Each one of us is concerned about Earth and its inhabitants. For some time there has been danger threatening, changes have begun upon the planet as you know, and there will be worse to come, but we will not dwell on this tonight.

As I left you last time, I mentioned that you and many thousands upon the Earth have dwelt on other planets in the past. I know that originally you were given knowledge that man appeared on this planet in the early days of Lemuria, the garden of Eden, and that he has existed upon this planet ever since, but as you know, as each incarnation goes by, the soul returns to the spirit world. During that time, there is a learning and resting period, and on returning to this planet, a decision has been made, a choice of what will be dealt with in that lifetime. Occasionally, the choice is made, or has been in the past to exist upon another planet, maybe this will be a new thought in your minds, but I think that it has been mentioned to you that Jesus has dwelt upon Venus at one stage in his incarnations.

Experience can be gained on other planets, because you become a different type of being as a result. It cannot be in human form necessarily, and as a result the experience is completely different. There is also a matter of free will; this does not always exist wherever we visit. Upon the Earth, man has free will as you know, but not on all the planets, and each one is in a different state of existence, a different state of life's experience. Some are extremely well developed through the mind, and the bodies are not so strong as yours. The minds are all powerful, and as a result, learning can be achieved at faster rates upon such planets, because with thought being all powerful, using a trained mind such as one living upon Andromeda, for instance, the mind can create many experiences for those who dwell upon it. There is no need to travel because the mind can do this through visualisation and teleportation, as you think of a place, there you are within that place, moved by the mind through thought.

Therefore, new experiences can be gained for people who have dwelt upon these planets, and they have that experience within their past lives. You yourself, Beryl, have lived upon Arcturus, as you know there is a twin soul living there at present, of which you are a part. Many people exist with their other half, shall we say, upon another planet, or within the world of spirit. Most beings have twin souls, therefore this is not unusual, each half of that soul is experiencing different lifetimes, different situations upon other planets at the same time.

Therefore there is much to learn upon this subject. Through past lives' experience upon other planets, learning how life exists on other worlds, can mean a great difference to a soul who is experiencing trouble on this planet, because suddenly a situation may arise, where the experience from that other planet can come into play and save the life of that individual, or those who dwell with that person. It may be a number of situations that have been experienced in the past. There is too much detail involved to elaborate on any particular situation, but as a result of experiencing these lifetimes on other planets, and meeting different denizens there, it means that we are all one. All are a part of God's creation, and now you realise how vast this life experience is, when you contemplate the number of planets that are available to live upon in different forms.

It makes you wonder and realise that there are endless possibilities for the future, because if this planet were to end its days, there would be facilities ready to disembark the entire inhabitants of the Earth, those who are ready, able and willing to face up to this reality. Naturally it could not be possible for people who are not ready to accept this idea. They would probably be completely unable to envisage such a thing happening, and could not possibly take it in their stride. But we are talking now of those like yourselves, who have been aware of their spirituality for some time, and the spirituality of all beings. It is this that separates you from those who will stay within a three dimensional realm, either upon this Earth or to return to spirit in this lifetime, and later reincarnating upon another three dimensional world, until they are ready to accept their capabilities, because everyone has the capability of reaching into the etheric realm, raising their consciousness and linking with those who would speak to them.

We have been communicating for years now with many groups of people throughout the Earth, and they, like you, accept the fact that the Earth is at a turning point. They accept the fact that beings from Sirius can come into their room and communicate with them. We have not been in your area for very long, only a short while before we began this talk. We are aware that you were hoping to begin promptly tonight, we can gather this from the distance upon our space ship, and can immediately teleport into your room, rather like they do in that programme you have watched, Star Trek. On a beam of light, that is all it is, but the molecular structure is moved from one dimension to another quite simply, and easily. These programmes that you and many millions have watched have been helpful to turn the minds around of those who are ready to accept these thoughts, to be aware that it is perfectly possible for space ships to travel to other planets, and to meet up with other beings who are not as you are.

It would be unthinkable for beings as human as you are to live upon our planet, because of the different atmosphere. Our bodies are of a lighter construction than yours, and this is why we are tall and slender, and have a different appearance. We are more ethereal and less solid than humanity on the Earth, because of the atmosphere being of a different quality to yours. It would not be suitable to be constructed as humans are, and certain planets have very small beings upon them. It is all a question of the density of the atmosphere, and the suitability of each being's build must be perfect for their planet. Therefore, if you were to visit Sirius, space suits would have to be made for you to be comfortable, and capable of breathing our atmosphere, as you are at present. Think as you have been told though, you are moving into a higher dimension, and therefore your bodies will be changed. At present you visualise that you will be as you are now, but changes will be made within and around, so that you will be capable of visiting many other planets that will be available to you when once you are raised into the fourth or fifth dimension.

This time is coming closer, and it is difficult to say exactly which year everything will take place, and we have been forecasting it for some time. Everything depends upon man's attitude towards the planet Earth, as to whether it is going to happen quickly or that it will take a number of years.

Within your community I am sure that there will be quite a number who are already aware that these changes are on the way, and those who have had symptoms of various kinds. Some have been affected rather powerfully by these changes, and I am speaking now of those who have had problems with their heart, or felt dizzy, or their heads have been aching much more than usual. All of these are linked with changes that are being brought about within your atmosphere. It should not affect you unduly; it just depends upon the physique of the individual.

Change is all about you, and it will be for the better in some ways, particularly if you are spiritually aware, as you and some of your friends are. Therefore, there is much to look forward to in the future, and we look forward to passing on further knowledge to you, and those with whom you are in touch. We will give you more knowledge next week. For the meantime, we give you our blessing and leave you now. God bless.

CHANNELLED COMMUNICATIONS FROM SIRIUS ORON-3

Greetings to you this night. It is good to speak to you again, and to visit your home. I greet you as a brother, and I hope that you will feel a similar attitude towards us. We still hope to give help to the Earth at this time. My ship is safely in the sky above, with a cloaking device; I think that is the term that is used in the programme you watch, and it simply means that it is invisible. It is rather a good way of putting it, because sometimes we decide to show ourselves, just from time to time, to let people know that we are around. It may be a comfort to some, but perhaps to others it will be frightening. It all depends on your attitude. I know that in the past, you have seen a space ship, and you were intrigued and interested, and this is how we like people to feel about us, to have wonder, and to feel a kinship towards us.

As I said, we are still hoping to help the earth dwellers, and to advise on various things that are happening at this time, or will be happening in future times. Already as you know, there have been earthquakes, floods and famine, also hurricanes and tidal waves, but this is just the beginning of change. I know that you have had these things before upon the Earth, but this is the beginning of the changes that we have mentioned, and we are hoping that you will be able to guide others who do not know of these things, when the proper changes come. It is a time of preparation, so that you and others like you will be able to warn those who are not aware of this, and help them in many ways. We, on the other hand, are preparing to equip our ships, so that we will be able to give practical help of various kinds. In fact, it may be feasible to fill several of our space ships with people, and take them onto our planet, or perhaps to a neighbouring one that is not so far away.

There are numerous systems of stars rather similar to your solar system, but not so far away as Sirius, and some of the planets have an atmosphere similar to the Earth at present, and although the changes will come about, so that the Earth herself will change, it may be a possibility that some people would wish to leave the planet Earth when these changes happen. I know that most of you who are aware will be perfectly all right, because you too will be changing as the Earth is changing. It all depends on the outlook, and certainly the people who would take advantage of us, giving them a ride to another planet, would have to be ready to accept this in their minds. So many people think of UFO's, as you call them, as flights of fancy, and they would consider it a flight of fancy to ride in a space ship, but others would be intrigued, and long to do so, as I think you yourself would. However, it will probably not be necessary for you, but we are just thinking of all eventualities, should the need arise. We will be ready with sufficient ships to help large numbers of people at the difficult time, when the catastrophe will no doubt strike.

We have been preaching this for many years, the fact that the changes are to come, and certain people have been waiting for something of this sort to occur. Others are just beginning to realise that it may happen sometime within the near future. So think on these things and allow your mind to get used to the thought that change is all around, and adaptation will have to be made. However, it is not the end of the world, shall we say, but just the beginning of a new Earth, with less limiting factors around, because you will be able to see many things that at present you cannot see.

We can see more than you can, and being from a planet of the fifth dimension, we can see spirit that is all around you, and it seems to us that it is real, but we realise that you cannot see it, or them, as the case may be. It is interesting, because we often see people around your house, not necessarily in the house, but wandering around your beautiful garden, and then we realise that they are not a part of your family, but perhaps they lived there many years back, and are still fond of this garden, and return to look at it. Perhaps they mingle with you from time to time, because we are not always around, of course, it is just that we are aware that these spirits are as alive as you are, just on another dimension. So many earth people seem to ignore the fact that they are spirit, and will return again. Once they have returned to their spirit world in the realms above, they will come back as another person, although the same spirit is there, as you know, just to experience another lifetime in a different place and with different people.

We also had this capability, but now it is unnecessary, we live forever as we are. You cannot see us, but we are as we always have been, although clothed in a more ethereal body, and as a result, we do not return to reincarnate, but continue on trying to be useful in this situation, always trying to do what we can to help other people on other planets besides Earth. We are attracted to certain planets to whom we have promised to give help, and as a result, we cover great distances between one planet and the next, of course. But as you know, the speed is very fast, and we can be back in the twinkling of an eye, from your planet to another, so that we can avoid having to spend a lot of time in space, as you call it. So, as a result, we do not waste time, but we can move very fast indeed. I think people have seen this happen, with space ships that have been observed from Earth. They have taken off reasonably slowly, and then just vanished from sight. They have accelerated so fast, that the eye could not follow them. It is rather, as they say in your programme, warp factor nine or similar, so that the acceleration is excessively fast.

So far, this has not been discovered upon the Earth. Progress has been made over the decades from the time when man first stepped upon his moon, and there was great excitement, because it was like discovering a new dimension, or should we say, rather like Columbus discovering America. It was something completely new, and from that time there have been great strides made. I think that man is trying to do his best, but there are still many things to be learnt to avoid polluting the Earth. I think that I have said before, that our planet Sirius has been affected in this way, in the past, and there is much to be done upon the Earth to eradicate pollution. There must be tremendous changes within peoples' life styles, and particularly industry, which is affecting rivers, and ships of all kinds have also polluted the oceans of the world. It is due mainly to oil, of course, when wrecked ships break up, or when a tanker is holed in some way.

All these things are most important to learn, and man has to recognise the fact that he should be preserving his planet, protecting it against pollution, and attempting to stop any nuclear problems also. This is important because when scientists split the atom, it was thought that this was a wonderful breakthrough, but it turned out to be a nightmare, because of its use for evil purposes instead. However, I know that governments are aware of this, and it is hoped that it will be overcome, so that the Earth will recover and be made fair once more. Mankind has great promise, and the young people of today are looking forward to a future when the Earth will be green and pleasant. They have much to look forward to, because, besides the fact that the Earth will be unpolluted in future days because of a different lifestyle, they will have a simpler and more direct life, linked with their spirituality, and linked with beings from planets that will contact the Earth in the future, rather as we are doing, and have done for many decades. Contact will be made possibly as a result of astronauts' work in the future. It is difficult to prophesy how these things will come about, there will be no confrontations because these beings are friendly, but there will be a coming together of the peoples of the Earth, and the beings from various other planets within the universe.

I know that their ships have been seen. They are slightly different from our own, and I know there have been sightings on more than one occasion, but I cannot say more than this. I think that the governments of your world keep many things quiet. They know about certain happenings, but do not wish to alarm anyone or cause distress in any way. There will be news of these sightings eventually, once people get accustomed to the idea of this possibility of linking with beings from other planets. I think that in the past, stories of sightings were hushed up considerably, so that the population of the Earth was unaware of many meetings with people who have actually spoken or had communication with beings from other planets. Quite often it has been in a desolate area, perhaps in a vast country like Russia, or in deserts. I know this has occurred, and eventually the stories will come out, but I am sure that most people will be very interested to hear of these meetings, and to learn more of the other beings who exist, and try to promote friendship between planets such as we are doing.

They only wish to help, and they know of the Earth's plight, and how there will be changes made, and I am sure that they, like us, will help anyone who wishes to remove themselves from the surface of the Earth in time to come. We are not saying that it will be impossible to live here. It will be possible for those who have learnt of their spiritual nature, and who are ready to move into a higher dimension. It is perhaps, those who are frightened of this, and need help of some kind, all will be well, we are just preparing your minds to these new thoughts. You will have plenty of notice, and we will be around to guide you, and to help in the preparation for the changes that will come. I know that your house here will be perfectly safe, and with warning, you will be able to cope, and be able to help others here. It may be that some will come and stay with you, and those of like mind will take neighbours in, family and friends if necessary. Do not fear, all will be well; we only want to reassure you of this. In the meantime, we give you our blessing, and we hope to speak of different things at our next meeting. God bless and keep you.

CHANNELLED COMMUNICATIONS FROM SIRIUS
ORON-4

I, Oron, greet you this night, and wish you well. My companions are here too, and we are all around you. You have been reading some articles from America that your daughter brought. Some of them sound rather alarming, of abductions and communicating with Earth dwellers. Perhaps certain people who come from the stars have a different outlook from ourselves, but we are gentle, and we can only speak to those who are open to our thoughts. Only speaking to those who wish to hear more from us, with advice and concern for you on the Earth. I am sure that you will keep an open mind on this subject, and particularly you will be pleased to know that you are perfectly safe, and will never be lifted into our spaceships without your consent. Perhaps in time you would care to visit a spaceship, but I know that you would like to consider this, and the time is not yet right for any of you to do so. However, you know that you would be perfectly safe if you were to join us for a short while.

It seems that others have been taken aboard spaceships in the past, and implanted with certain devices. The Siriuns would never consider this, and I think that it was perhaps something that has been blown up, shall we say. It may be part of someone's imagination, I do not know, but other space people or extra terrestrials, as you call us, who we know, would never dream of this either. Andromedans for instance, are also kindly people, so never fear, everything is well.

We come tonight to speak of the future, and the future for yourselves looks well, you have your place of peace, and you will be able to help many people in the future. The days of Earth's third dimensional situation are numbered. This is something that I know you and certain other people are aware of, but the numbers, although quite considerable, are not the large percentage of the Earth dwellers. Nonetheless, there are sufficient to pass on the message that you are gradually moving into another dimension, to pass on the message that you are gradually moving into another dimension, and in time this will be complete. As you know, you will eventually be moving into the fifth dimension, so it must be a gradual process, because you have to come to live out this stage of the Earth's development, as it moves two dimensions higher, after all the millennia that it existed on the third dimension, but preparations have been made and you will be joining us on our dimension.

As you have been told, it will be within the near future that you will be raised upwards to the fifth dimension, so your preparations should be made. You are thinking of growing more things yourselves, under cover possibly. As we warned you before, the changes will come and it may be difficult to procure food from elsewhere. It is a long term thought, but it is as well to have this in mind, so you will not go short of anything in the future. I think it is possible to store certain foods for several years, perhaps a year at least, and by this time, things should have returned to normal, as normal as conditions will be, and you will be able to procure food from the usual sources.

There are certain goods that will be unavailable, of course, and at that time you will find that you do not need them. As you have been told, the food that you will eat from that time onwards will be lighter, and you will find your needs are less. Drinking will be difficult, and water will be a precious commodity, so you should think if this as being a priority. Storage of water is always awkward, and it should be indoors of course, under cover of some kind, sealed off from the outside atmosphere. This is a difficult proposition I am sure, for you, but there will be an answer to it. If you do not find it, you will be given this, because we are helping as many people who are within our bounds as possible.

We will help in any way we can, but the future beyond that time is the one that I wish to speak on, because, as you know, your lives will be altered in many ways, and the people who will surround you will be those who will understand what life is about, and how they must evolve, and gain as much experience from their life as they can. Obviously, helping others to understand this, if they do not already. You will find that you will have a group of people surrounding you who are hungry for wisdom of all kinds, and you have within your house many books that will feed them this wisdom. It is like a search for the food of knowledge, and you must try to provide this, giving them spiritual nourishment of many kinds. Try to provide as much as you can, so that you have a good foundation of knowledge to give to them. You have been gradually collecting books, and have given some by your daughter, which will be most useful, and over the years to come, when time has changed everything, these books will be very precious to you, and those who will come to use them regularly.

So remember this, and try to garner as much of this spiritual food for others as you can. It is something that is important, and we will give you as much knowledge as we can from our side, our knowledge is gained from experience on our planet. We have gone through times of trouble, and have learned how to cope with this over the ages, and we too have learnt much, both from books and teachers of whom there are many on our planet. Rather like the Earth, we too have our Masters of the Hierarchy, and we have people who have learnt much from them over the centuries, and they have passed on their knowledge to generations of Siriuns. We have been a peaceful people, but we have been disrupted by catastrophes that have occurred periodically. They were not caused by violence, but natural disasters like earthquakes and floods, which occurred over the centuries, and we try to maintain an equilibrium that is difficult at times.

We have had problems in the past, but we have managed to overcome these, and now peace seems to be the norm. We have a different lifestyle from your own, but our teachers have taught us well, and we are beings of light as you are, learning spiritual truths, and we too are evolving as we should, attempting to learn the realities within a lifetime, the spiritual reality that is our inheritance as yours is, and we hope that there will be this same attitude from other well-known planets and their inhabitants. We are trying to work together with the Andromedans to help people on Earth, and they too have been encircling the Earth for some time, giving help where they can, and I think I mentioned before that if it was at all necessary, we would be here with our spaceships, to take aboard any who wish to leave the Earth at times of trouble. We do not foresee you having to leave, because it is only those who cannot cope who will have to leave when the dimensions have altered.

Those who are spiritually aware and have raised their consciousness to a higher level will remain upon the Earth. We have told you this before, but it is just to make it clear to anyone who is reading this for the first time, who has not heard previous communications. We hope that when things have settled down on your Earth, that there will be a new race of men creating a new Earth, with peace and the capability of maintaining that peace. Spreading it abroad, and men coming together as one, so that they can learn more about their real capabilities, those of their spiritual nature. That is the reality of life, and although at present you are living on a material world, it is still important to maintain your spiritual nature. This is the part of you that has always lived through the different incarnations, and this is the part of you that will continue on into the fifth dimension, and you will continue in this dimension always.

You will meet others, who you cannot see at present, and others you thought you would never see again, and you will be able to see us as we are now, who are completely different from yourselves. So your lives will be altered, and there is much to look forward to, as a result. There will be no fear of us, because you know that we mean well, and we hope that you will welcome us to the Earth, because we wish to bring more from our planet to help mankind when that time comes, and you are ready to receive us. We are not trying to colonise the Earth, only to help you in whatever ways we can. I think that then all men will understand this, and will gladly welcome us onto the planet to help, and perhaps when that time comes, we may offer to take man from time to time to visit other planets, because we have the technology to do so, within a very short space of time. Our ships will be ready to serve you whenever your wish.

There will be no problem about space travel in our ships, and instead of visiting places upon the Earth; you can visit other planets with ease. This is perhaps something to set a new trend of thinking. The present astronauts have had the occasional problem, but I think that this has been overcome, and you will find that man will be able to produce more spaceships that are easier to control, using different methods of transporting them through space. All these things for the future are new thoughts, and I think that man will develop many capabilities of travel, using different methods from spaceships, planes and cars. Also using the method of teleportation, and we have spoken of how we can beam into your room. These methods of transport are instantaneous, and man will eventually learn to use in the future, when he will be less physical, and slightly more amorphous in build. The new molecular structure will be such that all these things will be possible for you. We shall now leave it there, and I trust that our thoughts have been of interest to you, and will be to others in the future. We look forward to our next meeting with you, and we leave with our best wishes to your all. God bless.

CHANNELLED COMMUNICATIONS FROM SIRIUS
ORON-5

Oron of Space Command here. We greet you this evening, my two companions and I, who incidentally are members of my crew, and perhaps I should mention their names, they are Kroton and Sarmac. Yes, they are strange names I know, but nevertheless, they are Siriun, and we are happy to meet up with you once again, and to tell you more of our wisdom, we hope that you will be interested in what we have to say.

Our ship is presently stationed almost vertically above here, and it is very spacious, with many sections for different purposes within it. It is not a mother ship; it is purely to facilitate us to come nearer to Earth from the mother ship. Nevertheless, there are others aboard who are taking care of it at present. There are nine of us altogether aboard the ship, and there are facilities for all of us within that area. We use the smaller ships for moving shorter distances, that is from the Earth to our station within 'space' as you call it, which is many thousands of miles from where we are at present. Therefore it is good to have a base on mother ship that we return to quite regularly. Obviously we could not travel to Sirius very frequently, in fact we seldom go back to our home, and we do miss our home life, but that is our task, to try to pass on our thoughts and hopes for those upon Earth, and other planets who we are attempting to contact and help at this time. We hope that we will be of help, and we are dedicated in this work, it is part of the task we have chosen for ourselves.

In this work we acclimatise those upon Earth to link their minds with us, and once we have established that mind link, we are then able to direct the thoughts of those earth dwellers like you towards our life and ways of improving conditions, both upon the Earth and other planets. This is so that your thoughts are directed more outwards rather than inwards. I know that in meditation, you are hearing an inner thought, but it is the same when you hear me. I am speaking from within you somewhere, but I am also trying to make you think outwardly towards our spaceship, and the mother ship, our planet and other planets that are within your galaxy. I know that you have often looked upon the night sky and felt very small on seeing all the beautiful stars and planets that you can see from here on a clear night. You wonder sometimes whether there are beings upon those twinkling lights in the sky, and you would be surprised to know there are quite a number of inhabited planets and stars. You are aware now that Sirius is inhabited, as most stars are, by beings of a completely different nature from your own in build and in lifestyle, but I think that you would wish to know more of our life on Sirius.

When we were upon Sirius, before starting our journey to the Earth, we had training for the work in hand. We had trained previously, of course, in piloting vehicles, such as spaceships, but the extra training was to learn of how beings such as yourselves thought and lived. We already had a number living upon our planet, who had previously visited both Earth and the other planets, which we have attempted to contact, therefore, much was known about the Earth and the conditions upon it, and how the future of earth dwellers would be affected in times to come. Our teachers gave much knowledge to us, and we came well prepared. We have halls of learning upon Sirius in certain areas, like your towns or cities. We call them centres, and they have large areas that are inhabited by ourselves and by other beings who live upon our planet, who are not of the Siriun nationality, shall we say, but who have come to live on the planet and to serve us in certain ways.

They are not slaves, but workers who do manual work for the Siriuns. They are smaller than ourselves, and also slender, more slender than the earth dwellers, but they are from a neighbouring planet that has become extinct, and we withdrew them from there, at some stage in the past. I cannot remember how many years ago, quite some time, perhaps a hundred years or more, and they have been dwelling with us here, and are happy to do practical work, because their brains are not quite up to our standard of intellect, and therefore, it is ideal to have this work done for us, so that we can specialise in developing our intellect to a higher degree. They have their section of dwellings within the centre, and they come to work within the halls of learning, and our homes if we wish them to. Rather like you would have someone to clean your house, or work your garden, it is the same principle. They are, perhaps, your height or smaller, and they do much good for us, and are thankful to be upon our planet.

Our lives are genuinely good, in respect of the fact that there is no crime upon our planet at all, and therefore, there are few dangers, unlike the Earth at this time, where there is much violence. We are a peaceful people, and there is no violence here, so that young Siriuns can play contentedly, knowing that all is well, and all the parents can be assured that they are safe. Our planet has a different type of atmosphere, and we have very little greenery like the Earth. It is quite arid, and irrigation is required to enable us to grow various foodstuffs, the soil is rather a reddish gold colour, but it is quite fertile, and we grow many quite exotic fruits and vegetables of various kinds upon our own areas of ground. Sometimes we combine together in what you might call a commune, and several of the workers come and care for our plots of earth, so that they produce the food for us.

We are able to combine together in our dwellings, rather similar to your buildings that are made into flats. They are the same principle, but not quite so tall as some inn your main cities, and the centres are quite widespread. There are many thousands dwelling in one area or centre, which is much larger than your nearest large town, Newcastle, very widespread. Just the side north of the river, the main part of the town, is what I am speaking of, that is the size of the centre in which I live. I know that you cannot really imagine how it is with us, I am just giving you a rough idea to begin with, so that you may be able to visualise the conditions on our planet.

As I have said, we have had natural disasters in the past, but they appear to have been overcome, and everything is settled and calm, and the existence upon Sirius is pleasant. It is warm without it being over-hot for us, and as I say, there is water available within viaducts that cross over roadways, but they are not roads, as you would know them, they are walkways within our centre. We do not have cars and lorries as you do, so it is considerably quieter. The traffic is of a different kind, we have small vehicles that fly just above the ground, which will take two or three people from one place to another, just short distances. They are quite safe, and if we wish to walk, we do, but we do not need to concern ourselves too much with traffic, because it is minimal. The centre is not one that has space ships nearby. There is another centre some miles away that is designated rather like your airports are, as a landing zone for the spacecraft, but the smaller vehicles that we use upon the planet, we can park in our own garden areas. They are not called gardens, but it is the same principle, they surround our places of living.

There are different halls of learning, and the children go to education centres like your schools. They start learning from quite an early age, and they continue on learning in various stages to the age of about twenty, and then they are ready to start work. There are a variety of tasks that they can undertake, including training for spaceships, and for teaching of so many kinds. The children have a happy home life, and we try to return when we can, so that they can see us regularly. Sometimes it is almost a year before we return, and if the children are young, we really miss them, as you can imagine, but that is life, and we know that this also happens upon the Earth, when men have to go away as the sailors do, who said the seas of the Earth. I think your astronauts have strict training, which is similar to our own, and they have to be away from home for long periods of time. It is a similar life style upon their ships, and they will realise what it is like for us, who have greater distances to travel than them. We, who live upon Sirius, have been trained for so much longer, and have learnt over the centuries what they are beginning to learn now.

There has been so much evolvement over that time, both within Sirius, and other enlightened peoples like the Arcturians, and the Andromedans, and those from the Pleiades. All of them have been contacting earth dwellers for several decades, but within the last ten years, I would say that all of us have been more successful in reaching you with our thoughts. It is of concern to us that the earth dwellers must be prepared for future days, and I think that we have passed on this message quite firmly over the last few times we have spoken to you. We know that you have this in mind now, and hopefully you will pass on the same thoughts to others who understand, and who will attempt to prepare for the future, knowing as you do, what will be to come, and that preparations should be made for storing things that will be necessary for that time. We know that you are not entirely sure when the changes will come to the Earth, or what the conditions will be here, and none of us are certain about this. We only know that your life style will be altered, and simplified, and that you should have facilities for storing food for a length of time, and stock everything that would be essential to life for some time. Just in case you are not able to go out of doors, or very far from your home, so that you will have those facilities around you, and can bring in others to live in this place of safety, and encourage others to do the same if necessary.

    We had the same situation quite some time ago, and we know what it is like to have your life altered so dramatically, and we just hope that you will be completely ready when the time comes, with your store of food and water. It is always difficult to store any liquids in large quantities. I know that you have been discussing the ways and means to do so, and I am sure that you will come to a happy conclusion on this. We hope that you have been interested in hearing something of our life upon Sirius, and we will try to describe in more detail how our centres are arranged on the planet, and what our dwelling places are really like, next time we speak to you. In the meantime, we salute you, and leave you with our blessing this night.

CHANNELLED COMMUNICATIONS FROM SIRIUS
ORON-6

Oron of Space Command here. We greet you this night, Sarmac and I, together. There are only two of us this evening, and we hope we can have an interesting talk once more, partly about our planet, and conditions there, so that you may visualise how we live. I spoke last time on the Centres that we have. They are scattered over the planet rather similarly to your towns and cities, where the best locations are, both for irrigation, and for spacecraft landing, and setting forth. We have a planet that is of a different type to your own, it is not as mountainous as yours, there is not so much water upon it, but nevertheless, there are small seas and lakes, so that rivers and streams can produce the water required for the Centres.

We have in our Centre many places of interest, rather similar to your planet. We have theatres, and other means of entertaining, though we do not go out as you do, to dine with one another, because eating is less important to us than it is to the earth dwellers. As we have mentioned before, we do not need to eat so much as we used to, and consequently, our stature is slender. Some people may not be aware of our height, which is roughly six and a half to seven feet in your measurements, and we have plumed feathers sweeping backwards from our faces. We have rather bird like features, and we know you have been told this, but others who may read this book are not aware of it. Over the centuries we have altered slightly in appearance, as a result of our raising to a higher dimension some time ago, and therefore our bodies are not as solid as they were previously.

Our buildings have to have slightly higher ceilings than your own, and larger doors, and the windows are different from those upon your planet. They are thicker, because of the warmth on Sirius, it is very much warmer than on earth, and therefore our sun has to be obscured by tinted and thickened glass. We have to shelter from the sun more than you do, and therefore our clothes are suited for this, covering our limbs more than you do in summertime. This is advisable when you have a sun as strong as ours, and consequently, the houses look different from yours. The roofs are mainly flat, with a slight tilt towards front and back, not as steep as most of your buildings. They are more streamlined, and the windows run the length of the building with occasional support, and the doors are self opening and closing, like your shops, so it is easier for entry and exit when carrying things about, and can be locked.

The roads are not as wide as yours, because of the lack of vehicles, and we have viaducts carrying water across the roads, which lead to the fields beyond the Centre, and also to our dwelling areas where we also need some irrigation. Within the Centres many people throng to meet one another, in similar ways to those of you who live within towns on earth. We shop and like to meet up with one another after our work, because not everyone of course does the type of work that we do upon the space ships. There are many Centres located near our own, and we can travel to them on our small vehicles, or we can project ourselves as we do, from our ship into your room. Mostly we travel as family units, and can reach the next Centre within a very short space of time. As I said, the ground is fertile, and there is less greenery, but there are types of trees and bushes that grow in a less luxuriant fashion than those on earth, and there are flowers of many kinds, quite colourful, therefore, we are not devoid of plant life.

There are also animals of many kinds, domestic and wild, and our domesticated animals are different from your own. There are some that we have around our homes, like dogs or cats. We have these small creatures that are similar size to a small dog, and they have a coating of thin hair like a Jack Russell, they are smooth haired and do not feel the sun's heat too much as some of your thick furred ones. We have birds of many kinds, quite startling colours, and some of these dwell in our gardens, and during the day they are fed by our manual workers, therefore they are looked after by us occasionally, when they need help, but they find their own food most of the year.

We also have a cold season like your winter, when the sun is not as powerful, and the growing season abates, and we have to store things in the house for this time of the year, but it is not as cold as your winter, and we do not need fires as you do, we just have heating control to combat the colder weather. It is not as complicated as the heating systems in your country, and other cold regions on the earth. I hope this will be of interest to you and others.

We have insulation on our space ship against heat and cold, so that the atmosphere within the ship is just pleasantly warm, and have sufficient to keep us going with food and drink while we are on board, until we return to the Mother ship, which we do quite frequently. The Mother ship can take about twelve ships docking at the same time, so there is quite a large area allocated around the Mother ship for this purpose, so that supplies can be given, of varying kinds, food, drink and fuel energy are also provided. The energy is not like you have on earth, and the ships are energised for a day and a night, and then they are ready to take off once more to travel vast distances.

We have an advanced technological civilisation, and it is very difficult to explain to someone who has little knowledge of these things. Suffice to say, that in time those who deal with space ships on Earth will eventually find a new form of energy other than fossil fuels and man made capabilities. It is quite a different viewpoint, and I am sure in time that your scientists will come up with the same system as ours in due course. We use very little fuel when we are travelling these vast distances from one planet to another, and it is required that we jettison off from the Mother ship, and then drift through space at vast speeds.

We only need the fuel to start and end the journey, and when we stop above a planet, we have to use energy to arrest the flight, but once that is done, we are just stationed in space above the planet concerned.

Mostly, we make our ships invisible with a device that hides them from view, but from time to time, we show ourselves to humans and beings we visit on other planets. We feel it is important that people on all planets become used to seeing space ships, and become aware that other beings can visit without being a threat to them. So many people seem to feel frightened at the thought that other beings can land on their planet, and they assume that they will be attacked, and cannot conceive that they can be coming in love and friendship, trying to help in whatever way we can. It is just a question of people accepting what is to be, and then realising that all is well, and they need not worry. From time to time, over the decades, we have shown our ships, and sightings have been written up in books and newspapers, of extra terrestrials as you call us, and ships that have been seen, either in an ominous or friendly manner.

Now that people are gradually getting used to seeing space craft, we hope that this will be accepted and become the norm, because it is important that it does, so that when the time comes for your Earth to rise to a higher dimension, and help is required in certain places, we will be ready for this. We hope that by that time, those who dwell upon the Earth will be ready to accept us, and the ships will be less of a seven day wonder, but more a point of interest to all concerned. We hope you will look forward to seeing our ships around the planet, knowing that we will do no harm, and that perhaps when you see one from our planet, you will be able to point out that it is from Sirius, and that you know who is upon it. We only wish to help, and as you know, we have been preparing people's minds for the changes that will come, and part of your work will be in helping those around you with these changes in dimension and lifestyle.

The planet will become more temperate in general, so you will find it less cold here, and those places that are extremely warm will find it more pleasant to live there, when the changes occur. There will still be rain, which is necessary for your seas and rivers to remain constantly full. We did not mention that we also have rain; this is obvious now because I mentioned that we have seas, lakes, and rivers, but the rain is very precious. We try to conserve it in containers, which I am sure you will be doing at this time of change, and I hope you will be ready when the time comes. You know that you will be protected, and perhaps you will be able to advise many people on the situation, bringing it casually into conversations.

Several of our ships are stationed above your planet at this time, and a number of our people are contacting people like you, making them aware that we are here and ready to help at any time. If you wish to contact us, you only have to think of me, and I can be quite quickly with you in your room to speak to you if you need help for the work that is ahead, but I do not think this will be necessary. You will be given ample warning beforehand, and then be able to stock up on provisions in preparation. We salute you all this night, God bless.

CHANNELLED COMMUNICATIONS FROM SIRIUS ORON-7

Oron of Space Command here. We greet you this night to help you in our practical way. This is our task to help Earth dwellers. There are many star systems that are being looked after at this time, the Solar System is one that is our concern at present. Over the decades, we have been overseeing your planet, and now we feel we have made some headway. We have been influencing as many groups of people as we can, to spread the word regarding the future of the planet, it is something that is necessary at this time, in order that the Earth dwellers will have time to make plans for the future. It is best to be aware of the future and the changes to come, to not worry about it, but prepare for it.

In future days, your lives will be different from now, in practical ways, you will find that your houses will have to be used in a different manner than at present, because your heating systems will be null and void if you use electricity, gas or oil, and in time, any fossil fuel will be unreachable. Therefore, you will have to depend on wood for fires, if you need them, and you will ultimately need them for cooking, unless you eat raw food. This is at the time between the present conditions, and when the ultimate conditions take place. It will probably only be for a year or so, but it is as well to be ready, so that you do not get caught out in any way. Most people, who you are aware of, your friends and relations, will be perfectly safe in this area, and we are thinking of different areas around this part of the country, other than the south. We feel that the middle section of the country will be safe, comparatively, except for areas where there are rivers that are close to their embankments, like the Thames, low lying, because there could be considerable flooding. It is quite a possibility, and I think this must be considered for anyone who is either near a coastline or close to a river, unless they are on a hillside or there is a retaining wall. They should either build walls or try to move to higher ground, but it is difficult to generalise, but do make this known to others.

There is much to look forward to in the future, because when the Earth and yourselves move upwards and ascend to a higher dimension, you will find many benefits in time to come. You will see people who are in spirit as I have said; who you never thought you would see again, until you passed over to spirit. You will be able to see them once again, and this is a wonderful thing for those who have lost loved ones. I think you will be overjoyed to see certain ones whom you thought you would not see for many decades to come. There will be a change of appearance, because, as they are in spirit, their spirit bodies are refined and changed to look as they did in the prime of life. This is to be taken into consideration, perhaps you will not recognise them initially, and some of you may be nervous of this. There is no need to be, because your bodies will be more like your spirit bodies too, and they will just be clothed with a thin layer of flesh, shall we say, rather as we are. Being in the fifth dimension, we do not have such solid bodies as those in the third dimension, in which we were at one time. Therefore, we do not need to eat very much, as said before, but we have to take sufficient to keep us content. Once you have learnt to take in food and drink, unless you actually pass into spirit, and make that transition of dying, as you may call it, there is still the tendency to need food to fuel you, and make your life feel more fulfilled. It is necessary to replenish your bodies, recharging them, like our craft on the mother ships, which have crystals of a different kind to Earth, but they help to give energy to our spacecraft. We watch the Earth day and night, and hope in some small way to help you to look to the future, your own future and for the planet. We are helping Earth dwellers and those on other planets, but we have thoughts on others things this night besides your preparations for the future.

We hope you will be interested to hear of where we last landed, we were upon Mars. I think that the Earth dwellers had reckoned that no one could possibly live on Mars, and quite a number of Earth people were disappointed because they used to talk about men from Mars. The little green men who were seen periodically, and it seemed as though these stories must be wrong, if it was impossible to live there, but strangely enough there are little green people, beings who live on Mars. Of course, it had not been taken into consideration that they could be on another dimension, and also that they might dwell within the planet, rather than on the surface, as you do, and as a result, there is still much to be discovered about Mars, and other planets near you, or reasonably near you in your Solar System.

So take heart, and realise that it is perfectly possible that on many of these planets that are considered impossible to live on, it is possible to live within the planet, and there are systems of all kinds within many of these planets that seem unsuitable for life. Venus is another that appears to be hostile to life, and would be impossible for human life as it is at present, but consider different beings that are made up of gaseous substances or of a liquid rather like mercury. All things are possible; so do not be surprised that life is possible on Venus, but in a different shape, and on another dimension from your own.

Everything is possible if you think about it deeply, and I think you will find that many things you might have considered to be strange and rather laughable are perfectly true. Sometimes fact is stranger than fiction, and remember the saying, where there is smoke there is fire, and therefore the little green men that have been talked of are true. They are reality rather than fiction.

You will find as time progresses that you must keep an open mind on everything you read or speculate on, for you will realise that your minds were closed to those realities which is natural, because you have been brought up to think of everything as being as it is, here and now, but in the future it will be different, and you must consider this, that you will be on a higher dimension than you are presently, and at this level you will be able to see beings on other planets, rather like ourselves, who you will be able to see too. Perhaps you will see us before then if we allow you to, it is difficult because I think it takes time for Earth dwellers or anyone on the third dimension to visualise different beings without being frightened. Something that is completely different from your own humanity is always strange and rather fearsome, until you realise there is no harm in those beings, who only mean to help.

Always beware, because certain beings are not as kindly as we are. We will take care to advise you on this, should any who should be guarded against come near you, and we will be ready to guard you. Mostly, they are of gentle disposition, and mean well towards you upon the Earth. Recognise the fact that you are capable of learning much more about other civilisations and planets, and should be made aware of the many beings who cross space, the great vastnesses of space, in order to bring help to those on the third dimension. There are a number of ships that are on this mercy mission for Earth dwellers, and others who are ready to move upwards in the future. Most people do not know how this ascension can take place, and how this could come about in a short space of time, after all these centuries when the Earth has been three dimensional, since the early days. Those first days of mankind, and long before that of course, when the Earth was like a living volcano, and then cooled, and eventually life started upon it. All within the third dimension, and why should it be that it should move up two dimensions in a short space of time, but this is something that has to come about, and it is from now onwards that there will be many gales and climactic changes as been mentioned.

All this is part of the beginning of the changes, and it will be gradual so that you can adjust to it, and the beings from other planets are also spreading the word, to give hope and faith to those living on planets who are changing their ways, and people's lifestyles will of necessity change with the dimensions. Those who are helping besides the Siriuns are the Andromedans, and Pleiadeans, and there are also ships from Orion and Alpha Centauri, and others. Quite a number of planets where helpers have decided that this was their task in life, to enlighten the peoples whose planets are still third dimensional. We in particular are helping in a practical way to bring about this mind link with the Earth dwellers, and to pass on our knowledge of what will be in the future. The planet is not going to be devastated or have terrible tragedies. Everything will take place in due course, and you will be acclimatised to the idea soon.

All will be well, and we will be here to guide and help you periodically. We have described our planet to you, not in great detail, but just to give you a rough idea of the conditions on our planet, and the Centres in which we live there. The buildings are different in construction from yours, as our sun is extremely powerful, but life is pleasant there and peaceful. Those on our spacecraft wish you well now, and in the future, and hope that in time that you will visit our planet and see for yourselves how life is with us there, but only when in the fifth dimension, eventually. Our greetings to you and all who read this, we salute you this night and give you our best wishes for the future. God bless.

CHANNELLED COMMUNICATIONS FROM SIRIUS ORON-8

This is Oron of Space Command. Greetings to you this night from all three of us. We are happy to see you, and we hope we can talk freely to you about several subjects. One of these subjects is the linking of our minds with those on the Earth. We are finding that, as time progresses, there is a better flow of thought between our minds, so the linking is becoming closer, and I think that those on Earth are managing to raise their consciousness to our own, therefore it is easier to bring through our thoughts to your minds. Over the last few decades we have been attempting to communicate with various people in a number of countries, and we have also given them a little grace in between communications, perhaps a few months or a few years, and then we have returned as we have done with you, Beryl. But now we feel that it is important to link with all those with whom we began, to spread the word of the changes that occur.

You need not worry about these changes, and not to alarm anyone, but it is just to give a warning to many who are completely unaware. There will be those changes and a need to prepare for future days, so provide stocks of everything that you will require in normal living for perhaps a year or so, to have them ready in the house. In the future, after that time, things should have returned to near normal. We will not say complete normality, because there will be a change in communications throughout the world, your world of Terra Firma, the dear Earth that you have known all your lives will be altered, but not irrevocably.

You will find that life will be of a simpler nature, less sophisticated means of transport for the time being, and perhaps television and radio networks will have altered in that time during the change, but you too will have altered as I have said. There will be changes within your bodies because of the change in dimension upon the Earth, and you will come to this quite easily. It will be so gradual you will barely notice, but you will be like us, becoming gradually lighter and less solid, and the changes will come about when you are ready for them. Those who have decided they cannot accept these changes will have been moved to another dimension, because they will not be able to live in the finer vibratory level of the fourth and fifth dimensions, as we are living in presently.

As I have mentioned before, within that dimension, we are able to project ourselves by teleportation, so we arrive on a beam of light, and you too will be able to do this with practice of course. We can also appear and disappear whenever we wish. This is something that you may not have considered, but it means that if you do not wish to be seen, you can arrange your molecular structure so it is invisible, and there are many ways of doing this, but the time will come when you will be ready to accept what we tell you. It is a thought to consider for future days. Beings on the fifth dimension are not always seen around your planets, our spaceships have been seen periodically, but not always. We have our cloaking devices to cover our craft, as said, when we feel it is better to work in secret, otherwise it means that people panic on seeing us circling the Earth.

So it is over the decades, that we and others like us, have concealed our space vehicles from humanity quite considerably, just appearing periodically, but in due course we will be sighted more often because we wish to let humanity know we are only here to help, and if they are aware of this, they will feel more settled and content. So they will get used to seeing spacecraft overhead in your skies. I think you would accept this, not every day perhaps, just now and again, and so we will show ourselves to you now and again.

Perhaps sometime, you and your friends would like to ask us some questions at the end of our communications, so if this is something you would like, please prepare a list of questions that we hope we can answer for you. It would be worthwhile considering which questions will be important in the future, how life will be, or anything else you wish to know, we will be pleased to answer. In the meantime, we thought you might like to hear about certain things concerning our lives that would be of interest to you.

Periodically we meet up with beings from other planets on our mother ship. We take care not to clash with the ideas of those beings from the Pleiades or the Andromedans, or any on the other planets who are working in the same way as we are. Therefore, there are meetings on one or another of the mother ships. They also travel vast distances, and have a care for those on Earth and other planets of the Solar System, as well as other three-dimensional planets like yourselves with whom we are working. All of the planets mentioned have been working for decades as we have, preparing people for the future, so there is a linking of minds with all. We consider ways and means together, and make plans for now and the future for our mutual work. There are many beings with whom we come in contact, and we take care not to attempt work that they have planned to do. We compare one another's ideas, and we make plans, so they integrate well together. We always consider each other and it is important since we are working with the highest, such beings as Jesus and other Masters, who delegate to us what we are to do to help them.

Therefore, you must know that we have thoughts that link with God, so that we can help all beings at the highest level, and there is no unkindness. We work for good, and we know that the Arcturians and Andromedans, Pleiadeans and ones from Alpha Centauri, and others link together to work for the Masters of the Hierarchy, and in linking with them, we feel that we are doing whatever we can to work for the good of others. Our lives are dedicated to this, and the task ahead is something that we look forward to, because we think that in helping those who are a lower dimension than ourselves, we are doing whatever we can to raise and help them to understand how things will be for them in the future. We have also gone through this stage, many years ago, but as a result of having done so, we understand, and can explain it perhaps better than anyone else.

After our meetings with those from other planets, we are sometimes consigned to our home planet, and have time to dwell with our families. This time is very precious to us, and then after some weeks, as you call them, we return to our ships and join with others of like mind who are doing the work with us. Periodically we visit the mother ship, and collect information on the work ahead, and who we are to contact in the near future. We work together in our own spacecraft, usually any number from six to ten in each ship, and those with whom we work are also extremely dedicated and ready to do whatever is necessary for the good of the beings on other planets. We have dedicated our lives to this work, as I have said, and we enjoy visiting other planets and meeting people like yourselves who are attempting to help, linking with us for this work, and we are grateful to you for this mind link, and we hope that we will be able to continue with this for several years to come.

What is necessary now, is a dedication of more people who will link with us, and we hope to contact even more upon the Earth, and other three dimensional planets, so that the word can be spread more readily, because at times even if you try to spread this word to as many people as possible, it will not always be accepted if it is just hearsay from someone that you do not know, so that the more minds we are able to link with, the better, because then more people will know those who have heard directly from us, and this is better for us, for our work with you. If you know of anyone else who might be able to link with us, please ask them if they would be willing to do so. We will be ready to oblige if they will be prepared to hear from us. It is perfectly possible for anyone who is able to hear their guide, or that still small voice within, to link with us. We salute you this night, and we give you our blessing for now and the future. God Bless.

CHANNELLED COMMUNICATIONS FROM SIRIUS
ORON-9

This is Oron. We salute you this evening, and hope that we can have an informal talk about a variety of subjects. My title has changed a little since we spoke in your last house, but I wished to make it simpler for you, and therefore, I introduced myself as I had previously, of Space Command. Of recent times things have altered. There is a great Being of Light who rules over us, shall we say, and it is his command that we serve Ashtar Command, which has been heard of previously, in your country and elsewhere, but you had not heard of this and so I did not wish to confuse you. I must be truthful and tell you that this is my command now, and we are happy to serve under Ashtar for the rest of our lives.

We have been waiting for you for a little while, and now you are ready. You, like us, have had a busy day, although we do not call them days, they are just divisions of time, because man is the one who measures time so consistently and meticulously. Nevertheless, time is an endless belt, and we have spent that time busily, like you, but moving around in space. We have visited a group of people on another part of the world already, today, and spoken to them of many of the things that we have said to you. As a rule, the three of us come to your room as we have tonight, and we are happy to be here, it is time I think, to tell you of some things which may be of interest.

Regarding the changes, if you have no electricity now and again in the winter, it is important to have an alternative form of heat, such as a fire that does not depend on electricity, because oil boilers and ovens depend on electricity too, and therefore particularly in the country, it is important to be able to use solid fuel at times. In the future it may be that you will not need this for warmth, purely for cooking. We hope it will be so, because we know that you feel the cold here when the snow falls and the ice forms. We do not have this on our planet, it can become cooler, though, but not as cold as you have, but in the future your climate will alter with milder winters. There will be no extremes in temperature, and there will be less extreme between the poles and the equator, everything will be more equable, I think would be the word to use.

We hope there will be a time of complete peace all over the world and that wars will cease, we hope for this. It seems as though there never has been peace for hundreds of years, but I think that just prior to the changes beginning, there will be a cessation of war, and men will live in unity, and attempt to be as brothers to one another. This is what God requires of man. It is what the Master Jesus has hoped for man since His death, or rather, transition. But it has not occurred despite His efforts over the centuries, and those efforts of many saints, and others in the spirit world, who come and go, but are really present always, being the Masters who are part of the White Brotherhood.

I am getting off the subject; I hoped to tell you more about how your lives will be in the future. You will find that life will be simpler and you will live closer to nature for quite a while. I think that young people will help the older ones to cope through this time, because they will be capable of doing more physical work than the elderly, but it is surprising how those who are fit will be capable of doing, more than they imagined, and will enjoy doing so, given some rest time. You will find that those who have horses of any kind, will be in great demand, because there will be no oil or petrol available for your cars, so other forms of transport will be necessary. Perhaps you might like to invest in a bicycle! I do not know whether this is worthwhile, I am sure that you will manage until the time comes, when other transport will be available to you. I think everyone will have to learn to be more self sufficient in the years to come. Growing their own food under cover, and coping with everything themselves, rather than going to shops for some time to come. I know that you have this in mind, and will pass on this message to others to stock up on tinned and dried foods that will store for a year or two.

You will find that people will begin trying to reach churches to pray to God for help and guidance. People always turn to God in times of trouble or change, and I think you will find that people will be ready to learn meditation as well as prayer. It will be quieter with no heavy traffic on the roads, and you will have the time and ability to meditate peacefully for some time to come. This can be taught, and I think that people will be more ready to learn, because of course, those who are left in the fourth dimension will have accepted this, and be enthusiastic about joining in with your work, and reading books on many subjects that you have, and some of your friends also. You will be able to lend them to those who are not quite so far along the path as yourselves. All this will be of great interest to you, I hope, and I know that you will be prepared for it, because it is at the time of the changes that you will all come into your own to be of assistance to anyone who is wanting to learn more, and also to guide them in how they should prepare for that time.

I think that when the time comes, everyone will be ready to help one another, and join forces in many things, more so than usual, in a more natural, friendly way, rather like mankind was originally, before he became too 'civilised', shall we say. We will be available at all times, and if necessary we will be happy to arrange some kind of signal if you will be needing help of any kind. We will be watching over you always, as much as we can, of course, because although the Earth is changing, there are other planets in the Solar System and elsewhere that are also three dimensional, who will be raising up to the fourth and fifth dimension when you do. So we are taking care of millions on Earth, and on other planets who need help, and as we know that you are well prepared in thought now, we go on to help many more who have not reached that stage yet. Fairly soon we will not be speaking to you quite so frequently, but will reappear now and again, and will arrange these details later. Suffice to say, we know that in the future, we will be prepared, and those from other planets who are on our dimension will be helping too, so if not ourselves, the Andromedans or Alpha Centaurians or members of other planets who also do this work will be available for anything should you need it.

We know the time is approaching for your celebration of the birth of Jesus Christ, and we know that you have families who come together at this time throughout the world. If they are apart, they visit with one another, and I wish you all well at this time, and hope that it is a happy and uplifting time for you. I am sure that everything you do will be done with love, and I hope in the future there will be more appreciation of the Master Jesus, and the work that He has done over the centuries. He has communicated with many on the Earth in this way, and He has appeared to others in places such as the high mountain areas in the Far East. There are groups of monks and people living there who have been visited by Him, and other High Beings. He has done so much for Christian people and others over this time, and for many lifetimes before the one He lived in Palestine. We have known and loved Him for long, and we link with Him in our work.

We wish you well at this Christmas time, and we send our love and blessings to all. We will speak again very soon, God bless.

CHANNELLED COMMUNICATIONS FROM SIRIUS ORON-10

Yes, this is Oron of Ashtar Command. We three are all with you in the room this evening, and we give you our greetings this night. All is well, and we have been proceeding around the Earth today, watching over all the many places we visit. They are quite widespread, and it seems as though there are very few within Britain, perhaps half a dozen with whom we actually communicate. There are many throughout the American continent, where there are so many power centres, where people cluster and are enlightened. This has been happening over the last ten years, people within the continent of North America have been learning so much more about their own country, and becoming aware of those power centres, and visiting to meditate upon them. Many people visit these places, where there is so much power, raw energy that has been building up over the many centuries since America was first discovered.

The Indian population have a lot to do with this. They have dwelt close to the Earth, and their ancestors have been buried in these places of power. They have built up a tremendous force in these areas, and as a result, the ensuing generations have gathered together in these areas, and built up a spirituality that is second to none. Over the centuries, white men have exploited the Red Indians, as you are aware, and it is sad to think that many of these tribes are purely spiritual people. There have no wish to fight and kill other people, they just wish to live in harmony with their surroundings, and some of these have done so, but so many have been moved away from their own 'happy hunting grounds', shall we say. They have been shepherded across the plains, and taken to encampments that are not their normal living conditions. In the past, much has been done in the name of exploration, and the white men who have killed many of these people have a lot to answer for. Nowadays of course, things have altered, and many of these Indian tribes have become more civilised, shall we say, living in small towns around the areas where they originated, and have made different lives for themselves, doing craftwork, and using their many skills to advantage. It is not in the way they did it in the past, but at least they have been allowed to start again, whereas others who were exploited originally were not allowed to do so.

I am leading up to the fact that certain areas in America have these places where much power has accumulated, and around these areas there are groups of people who are learning much about capabilities they could never have known of a few decades ago. There have always been certain groups of people who were spiritually aware, but they have become much more widespread, and much is being learnt from books, workshops and meetings. As you know, it is the most important part of your life, your spiritual nature, to evolve your soul in each lifetime. We have been aware of this for so long, and as a result, our civilisation has extended our consciousness upwards, and this has become of great importance over recent centuries. As a result, we are beings of light, living upon the fifth dimension, as I have said, and we try to extend our knowledge constantly. Also, we continue our work in communicating with others like yourselves to impart our knowledge.

Living as we do in another dimension, it is difficult to talk unless we find someone who can channel our thoughts. It is difficult to pass on this knowledge to those on the third dimension who cannot see us, and therefore might think of us as being gods! As you with your different religions have faith in your God, you cannot see Him, but you know He is there. You worship, praise and pray to Him, and in a way, as we cannot be seen, we could be looked up to as gods if you were not to realise that we were beings like yourselves. Just because you cannot see us, it does not mean that we are infinitely higher than you, and should not be regarded as such. We only wish to pass on much of our knowledge to humanity, and beings on other planets. As you know, all of you are beings of light if your regard your inner self as a part of God, the divine spark that resides in you and within all people. Think of yourselves as beings of light and which will become brighter, and you will be able to gradually raise your consciousness, and eventually your bodies onto a higher level.

The changes can make you feel it within you, a different feeling in your heads, perhaps. Sometimes being quite painful or throbbing, especially the top of the head, as you become more sensitive to the realities of your capability of linking with those of higher worlds. The crown chakra is that part of you that makes you aware that you are spiritual. At times that area is quite sensitive and throbbing, and at times like that when you feel this sensation, try to sit quietly and raise your consciousness, so that you attempt to listen with that inner ear, and perhaps you will surprise yourselves. It is good to say a prayer before doing this, to ensure whoever speaks to you is of the Christ Consciousness. I know that most of you are aware of this, and make sure you are protected by prayer and surrounding yourself with light. In this way you can never be approached by any being who is not of the Christ Consciousness.

Over this time, there have been changes within people's bodies, quite subtle, but changes are occurring to prepare you for this rise into the fourth dimension, and eventually the fifth. The Earth has been experiencing climate changes, and of course the polar ice cap melt will affect low lying land, but there may be other changes that may counteract this in due course.

The Siriuns have been working together with other beings from planets that are evolved like us. The Andromedans, Alpha Centaurians, Arcturians and Pleiadeans are the mainstream of beings who are helping at this time. You may find you will be visited by some of the others now and again. I am sure you will make them welcome as you have with us, and we have always been made to feel pleasure when we meet you, and we know you feel likewise, because we are here to help you, and to try and guide you through these times. I am not saying it will be very difficult, because once you have warning, you are half prepared, and you know what to provide for yourselves, materially.

Try to pass on these messages to as many people as you can, particularly those who you feel are interested. We feel there must be many groups of people who will be interested in their own future, and the future of their families. We are on your side, our ships will be here to help if necessary, but we feel sure that this will not be necessary at the time. Everything is going according to plan, and as you know, we work with the Masters of the Hierarchy, especially Master Jesus, and we feel sure that whatever is done in His name has God's blessing upon it. We salute you and look forward to our next meeting. God bless and keep you all.

CHANNELLED COMMUNICATIONS FROM SIRIUS
ORON-11

Yes it is I, Oron of Ashtar Command who speaks with you this night. We are all here in the room with you, and are sending forth love towards you. We wish you all well, and we have words of wisdom we hope to speak to you tonight. Always we feel a bond towards you, and I think you feel the same. I know that you wish you could see us, and perhaps in time you will. There is still much for mankind to learn in each lifetime, which is why you incarnate, as you know. Upliftment of the spirit is of vital importance. This is something that we learnt many hundreds of years ago, because, as you know, we are on a higher dimension, and have learnt and evolved over those centuries, always attempting to improve our capabilities, and know you are doing, and many others too to improve their lot. We hope to help you.

You are receiving teachings from the Masters, and you now appreciate how similar our communications are. It is of interest to find that we tally in many ways, and we always exhort you to raise your consciousness higher, in the same way that the Masters are attempting to do so with those teachings for mankind. It is only through this that your spirituality can come to the fore, something that many never learn. It takes so many incarnations for them to be awakened. To us they appear to be asleep, because they seem to go around in a dream, unaware that half of their reality exists. If we were to go upto them and try to speak to them, they would be completely unaware that we were here. They would never tune into our thoughts, or be aware that anything is different. They would probably never see the spacecraft if it were right in front of them, I may appear to be mocking, but it is the truth, and there are so many who just live a life unaware of their spirituality. Living on the material plane of existence of thinking, and never attempting to reach any higher than they are. They will take a long time to rise to the fourth dimension, when changes come to the Earth, and will be swept onto a third dimensional world when changes come.

However, many others are learning and will do well. They have an attitude with an open mind and eagerness to learn more than they know at present. This is good, and it shows they are ready and able to lift onto the next dimension, and they will profit well by this and find it easy. The transitional time between the third and fourth dimensions will seem quite simple, as it should to all who are on the spiritual path. The changes will be dependent on man's attitude to one another.

The forces of the lower astral dimension seem to be pulling many who are of a violent nature, full of fear and negativity, and they have been affected by evil and elemental beings who live on the lower astral dimension. These beings can have an effect on some people's base nature if they have not achieved a very high level of thought, they can be dragged down and become fearful as well as negative. If you encounter anyone like this, arm yourself with your own protection, throwing a light around you of the Christ Star, and with your armour of light you will always be protected against negativity, and send forth light towards those who are of this negative outlook. You can come across such people in your daily lives. You may pass them on the street, and you can sense a different atmosphere around them, like a black cloud, if you are sensitive. So it is important to positive in your thoughts, in your lives.

Positivity should be nurtured, and particularly if you are sending healing light to other people. Try to visualise them looking well and happy, with light surrounding them, and send positive thoughts as well as projecting healing into them. In this way with these positive healing thoughts, you can help many people even if you know very little about healing itself. The visualisation, positivity, light and love are all beneficial, and will serve to help them in many ways. They can rise to a level where they can be given healing, and it is often when people are feeling a little down that they tend to become ill, because their inner light that is of God, is not as powerful as usual.

It is strange how a little negativity can cause more problems, and it is only when you reflect on these things that you will realise it is so. If you know of anyone affected in this way, you can send light and healing thoughts towards them, and in this way you are helping people in your life. It is good to be able to do this, and is part of your life experience. Even listening to someone who wants to talk about their troubles can be healing, offering your sympathy can help to heal, and the problem eases when it is shared.

You need never hold all the problems you have on your shoulders, but can ask God to help you, for He is there to guide and help at any time, so if you do have a serious problem, tell God about it, and then it has been shared. Ask Him to take it, so you aren't weighed down by it, and avoid becoming ill. Remember this, as it is useful to know, for you can speak to Him in your mind, and even if not solved immediately, you will have lightened the load somewhat. It is part of life's experience to learn to cope with problems of many kinds, and you could not learn much in a lifetime of everything went according to plan with no problems, no worries, no negativity at all. It is through facing upto problems of life, you will become a better person as a result, and able to understand other people's problems as you have faced up to similar ones yourself.

There is much in a lifetime to help others, as we are helping those on other planets surmount larger problems when the time comes for that transition. This is something that we are here to assist you with, as are others from Arcturus, the Pleiades, Alpha Centauri and other friendly beings are also attuning to people on Earth and other three dimensional planets.

There will be many more communications in the future from us, and perhaps you may have some questions to ask the next time, and we will be happy to answer. In the meantime we salute you and send you our love and blessings this night. God bless.

CHANNELLED COMMUNICATIONS FROM SIRIUS ORON-12

Greetings to you both this night from us all. We know that this is the last chapter of the series, and you have some questions to ask at the end, so we will try to resolve what we have to say reasonably quickly for you. We have covered a number of subjects during these twelve communications, and hope to answer a number of queries you may have had about our lives, and your lives to come. What is important is the link between us that will not be broken, and can always contact us if you can reach our wavelength. We are in contact with more people who can be given instructions also.

We Siriuns have assisted various civilisations in the past, one of which existed and arose not long after the Atlantean disaster. We were aware of those on Atlantis, and knew there would be a cataclysm of enormous size, and so we were able to help groups of spiritually minded people at that time by transporting them to African shores. We helped man build the first pyramid and gave our knowledge to them, and the Pyramids and Stonehenge are linked on some way. There are many other points on the globe that link to the stars, which have taught man many things, and civilisations produced calendars, and knowledge has been learnt and re-learnt. So there is more to be learnt in future times.

So we have helped to build new civilisations from time to time, both on the Earth and other worlds, where groundwork was necessary to create wisdom for those who could accept it. We are happy to be available and capable of doing this work to help those less evolved civilisations on other planets, including Earth.

In time there will be a new order, and when the changes have come about, and humanity has settled down to a new altered lifestyle, we will help in any way to establish a stable existence on the Earth. We will fit in with all nations and it will not be know that we are from another planet, and become 'humanised' shall we say, so that no one would be aware we are from another planet. We shall be at the right place, at the right time to create this foundation for a new beginning.

When Atlantis was engulfed by the ocean, we disguised ourselves as humans, so that we would not be distinguished in any way, but would be able to fit in with all who lived at that time, including our clothing, and will be so in the future.

We will not be speaking to you for a little while after tonight, but will keep in touch periodically. Others will contact from other planets, I am sure, and perhaps in time we can all compare notes with one another, and maybe at some time in the future we can have a communication including beings from two different planets in one evening. This should be a point of great interest to you, and we can all unite in thought and word together. Perhaps in time you may see us, and I know it would be a wonderful thing for you, as you have tried to visualise what we look like. You know we are tall and slightly bird like, but it is a different thing to see someone instead of a mere description.

In the meantime we wish you all well, and give you our blessing this night, for now and the future, and we look forward to answering your questions. God bless.

CHANNELLED COMMUNICATIONS FROM SIRIUS, ARCTURUS, PLEIADES, & BETELGEUSE

SECTION TWO
ARCTURUS

CHANNELLED COMMUNICATION FROM ARCTURUS

Section Two

CONTENTS   **Page**

Section 1 – Arbul	49
Section 2 – Arbul	53
Section 3 – Arbul	57
Section 4 – Arbul	60
Section 5 – Arbul	63
Section 6 – Arbul	67
Section 7 – Arbul	71
Section 8 – Arbul	75
Section 9 – Arbul	78
Section 10 – Arbul	81
Section 11 – Arbul	84
Section 12 – Arbul	87

Channelled by Beryl Charnley

CHANNELLED COMMUNICATIONS FROM ARCTURUS
ARBUL-1

Let us begin, I am Arbul and I come from Arcturus. I am ready to establish communication with you, and I hope that we will have a successful talk together, because unless I project thoughts into your mind, we cannot communicate. All will be well, never fear. There have been communications, as you know, between the Arcturians and those upon Earth, because you read the book some time ago called 'We the Arcturians', and I know that you were interested in it. You read it rather quickly, and I think that you would wish to re-read this now. It is better though to have an open mind, than to have any set ideas of what may be said to you.

Our planet has had many dealings with the Earth and other planets of three-dimensional being, over the aeons. We are further on the path to evolvement. Our technology is way ahead of yours; although the Earth dwellers are beginning to 'take off' shall I say, at quite a pace. Over the last decade there has been a change in your outlook in creating many technological products, and I know that, although you are unaware of these things, perhaps, your children are more 'into this' as they say. Computers, fax machines and many other means of communication have been produced and improved upon over these last few years, and mankind has learnt how to make these things smaller as time progresses. Also, the machine that you use to speak upon is microscopic compared with the original means of communication on tape. They were very large and unwieldy, so try to imagine how it is with our technological products. They have become smaller and smaller as we have managed to make them more portable, and capable of producing communication for many hours on end, rather than perhaps thirty minutes, as your machine will do.

Nevertheless, the Earth dwellers have done well in learning very much more of these skills in the last few years, and I know that as time progresses, all these products will be made even more portable, and capable of producing communication that will be accurate and of very good sound.

My mind must be controlled so that your mind and voice can produce the words that I create at a speed that suits you, rather than whirling on at the pace that I am more used to doing. I knew that you were aware of this, and rather hesitant about communicating, but we can produce our thoughts so that they tally more, and that the speed of my mind is slowed down to the speed of Earth dwellers. Sometimes we find it difficult to hear your communications because they go so slowly, compared with our minds. You can compare this with small insects that fly at great speed, and have a high-pitched buzz. Were you to slow them down, the buzz would sound more like a voice, and the speed would be more your own speed, perhaps the little people could be compared with us. This is why you cannot see them unless you are very fortunate, because they are on a much higher vibratory level than you are, as we are on the fifth dimension, but think how it will be in time when you have raised yourselves to a higher level of being. You too will sound, as we do, like the insects and little people. Just think, your minds will be speeding along at a rate of knots, compared with now, and your voices too will sound fast, and unlike your own at present, rather like when you speed the tape up and sound like a chipmunk, as you often think and laugh about, but it is true. It is only a matter of working out the vibratory level, and you will realise then if you could speed up your talking on the machine, you too would be rather like the fly or the bee that buzzes along, and the sound would be not unlike that.

However, I digress. I am only trying to make you understand that it is more difficult to speak to someone who is at a much slower vibratory level, and I must need to alter the speed of my thinking to your speed. It is not that you are slow, compared with other humans, you are just the same as most, but I realise that our minds are faster, and we talk faster, and therefore we must try to level our speeds so that they are equal. Try to imagine how it will be in the future, and picture yourselves once you have raised your consciousness, and being on to the fourth dimension, and ultimately the fifth, so that in time you will be able to see and hear us, and we will be able to communicate face to face. This will be a wonderful thing, because as you know, you have lived on Arcturus at one time. You do not remember this, but I do, and others too have been either on Arcturus or other fifth dimensional planets, and have experienced life there for a lifetime, one incarnation either long or short, but nevertheless you have had that experience, and therefore your soul knows this, even though you, the person who is incarnating at present does not remember.

There are many at present incarnating on the Earth, who have had experiences such as this, and also a very much earlier incarnation. One of your first incarnations was upon Atlantis, as many who are reincarnating at this time were also, and are now back to help to bring into being a new way of thinking, and to help others at present to understand what will be occurring soon, the rising up into the fourth dimension. Some people need help at this time, and it falls upon you to try to explain and help them. I know that you, amongst others are ready to do this work, although you are not absolutely certain what exactly will occur when the Earth changes come about. You know that nothing disastrous will happen to you, or those whom you love, and other people whom you know who are on this spiritual path at present. You have been told that you will be under God's protection, and I am certain that this will be so. There are quite a few people that you know who were also incarnating on Atlantis, either when you were, or at an earlier or later date, and these Atlanteans have much to do at this time in the Earth's history.

I too, lived on Atlantis, and took part in many experiments there, both in healing and in seeing into the future. Much was known then, which has been lost to humanity, and other beings. There were crystals used then for healing, and for many things, and it is only now over recent times that humanity is beginning to use crystals again. There is much to be relearned on this crystal work, and I know that you have books on the subject that you are beginning to read. You are rather tentative about using crystals for healing, and this is quite right, because you must be aware of what you are doing. There is no harm in having a cluster of amethyst crystals under the chair of one you are healing. They are there to help to bring about good successful healing, and will be quite harmless, even if you know not what you do. It is the crystals that you use in your hands that you must be aware of how to use. So learn what you can, because they can be most useful, and accentuate any capabilities you have in the healing line. The abilities of those at present attempting to heal are quite powerful at times, and if you tune to your Higher Self or the Source of all Being, you can do no harm. If you have compassion and love for others, then it can only do good. We, ourselves, have healed over the centuries, and we know that spiritual healing can be very successful, when allopathic healing has sometimes failed. As a general rule, many people who have tried many cures from doctors and specialists finally resort to spiritual healers who can often heal someone who has gone beyond hope. Therefore, never lose hope; always have faith that you can do great things through healing, natural healing in this way.

The Arcturians can teach you much, and we hope that we can help you in many ways over the next few weeks, when I communicate with you. I have come to you on a beam of light from my space ship, as you call them, it is not far from here, but you could not see it as it is on the fifth dimension. There are others within that ship watching us at present, who are interested in everything that is happening at this time, because I have not done anything of this kind before. It is my first venture into communication with Earth dwellers. As I said at the beginning, Arcturians have been in contact with the Earth over the millennia, although perhaps it has only recently come to be known. I know others who have communicated with people on the Earth, and it is only through my knowledge that you were capable of receiving messages from other beings, either spiritual beings such as the Masters, or you have spoken to one who is within the Ashtar Command, and this is how I felt that perhaps I could communicate with you also. As we knew one another in a past life, I am aware of this though you were not, but are very eager to receive any message from our planet, and I am sure that I will be able to contact you regularly in order to give you information, both about our work, and the future of your planet, and those upon it.

I hope that my communication will be of interest to others. We pride ourselves on our independence, our hard work and integrity, and I am sure that you too are of a similar nature. I know that you have a conscientious attitude towards your channelling work, and I feel that whatever I say will be passed on truthfully onto the tape. My companions on my ship are extremely interested also, and they too will be taping my talk with you, because although it is your voice they are my thoughts, and perhaps it will be strange to them to hear your voice speaking my thoughts as the communication goes on. We have much information to pass to you, and this is a preliminary communication, so that we can find an adjustment between our minds. I think that we have achieved this, and I am very pleased that we have been able to talk together in this way. Next time I speak to you, I hope to give you more information, but for now, I will say farewell to all, and give my blessing to those who will receive this communication.

This is Arbul speaking to you this night. God bless.

CHANNELLED COMMUNICATIONS FROM ARCTURUS ARBUL-2

This is Arbul, and I give you my greetings this night. I come with pleasure to enjoin my thoughts with yours. What is necessary I now know is a slowing down of my vibratory level, to make it equal with your own. We, as I said before, are on a higher frequency, and it takes a little time to adjust to this. I hope that I can give you more information, and I wish to explain various things to you in the course of time. Our civilisation has been on the fifth dimension for thousands of years. We rose upwards onto this dimension, and at that time were helped by beings from other planets, rather similar to the way in which we are helping the Earth dwellers at this time. Each planet has its own idea of what is right, and we realise that our thoughts are not the same as your own. It would be impossible for dwellers on different planets to have exactly the same outlook on various situations. At the time we had our transition, we were helped by beings from Alpha Centauri, amongst others, and we realise what it is that you are beginning to appreciate.

We had similar feelings to yourselves at that time, and as you rise to a higher dimension, there are times when you wonder what is wrong, from time to time. Perhaps you may have odd symptoms that you have not had before, such as head pain, which I am aware you have just received, and you have been noticing this occasionally. I think others may be similar to you, or have had other sensations that they have not had before, only a temporary basis, but it is an adjustment of your body to ready you for the change in your vibratory level. So do not worry, it is not symptomatic of some dread disease that you and others may be considering. Know that this will be happening for some time, so do not concern yourselves unduly. We went through this, and many other symptoms, and we were given great assistance by those beings from Alpha Centauri, and they described to us what we might have to expect in the transition stage.

It is difficult I know to appreciate this, and not to know the exact timing, because once you are on the fifth dimension, time does not exist. We have experienced the difference, and realise how you have been ruled by time since the first clocks were made, and it was man himself who created this. We appreciate it because we were of a similar outlook then, and we know that each day is ruled by time, twenty four hours in each day, divided into sections by yourselves into sleeping and working, and the times you eat. Everything is taken into consideration, but once your bodies have adjusted, and you move into the higher dimensions, then there is no necessity for this, and you will find many benefits that you cannot imagine at present, but just try to visualise how it will be when you do not have to be at a certain place at a particular time. There will be so many changes that you cannot yet realise, but we understand this.

We know that your methods of transport also will be altered in time to come. Your fossil fuels will gradually be phased out, and will be unnecessary for future travel, because there will be new discoveries made in this, and you should realise that the transportation of our spacecraft is completely different from the spacecraft that are used by Earth dwellers. Your astronauts are subjected to great pressures by the very method used in escaping from the Earth's gravity pull, and a great amount of fuel expended in the way that your craft are sent out into space at present, but try to visualise how it will be in the future when other methods are available to you. Some craft use quartz crystals, utilised in a certain way that will eventually be discovered, but also consider that we can teleport ourselves from one place to another on our planet. So try to visualise how it will be for us in our craft if you magnify that in a way to move our craft. I cannot go into more detail, but we have on board many methods of moving the craft.

We are insulated against the different temperatures involved in transport, because we travel at such a rate that you can visualise, that the speed would create friction if you were moving at that speed normally, especially near the sun or other planets with great heat, it would be impossible to keep the craft in one piece. We have overcome this in many ways, and our comfort is assured, we do not fear anything in space, as you call it, and we are comfortable and well supplied with everything that we need. Large stocks of food and liquid are unnecessary for us, because we do not eat and drink as much as we did, when we were three-dimensional like yourselves. Our bodies have adjusted and evolved in a different way, and therefore, we only have supplies to cater for very few wants on our behalf, just when we feel inclined to have a break for refreshment, but we do not use so much energy as you do, and we do not have the same needs as we had before.

Our civilisation has expanded and improved over the last few thousand years, so that there is peace among its inhabitants. Expansion of consciousness is what I am talking about, so that we are on a different wave band from your own. We have used telepathy in order to create new thoughts, and we utilise telepathy in teaching all pupils who are educated to a high degree. All of us are of one accord, we act as one and we do not individualise our activities, so that as a result we try to create situations that will benefit the whole of our civilisation. All the citizens of each section of Arcturus work together, so that they work for the good of all. We try to help one another in this way, so that each one reaches the same degree of capability, raising the consciousness of all to a high level, and our only thought is to serve those who we honour, and who run our civilisation. Elder brethren who are beings of great experience, rather like the Masters that you look up to, we try to work together as one in order to serve all, and the Masters who serve the whole of creation. We also look up to and try to work in unison with Them. All beings who are of like mind in our fifth dimension work for the Masters of the Hierarchy, and we live only to serve, and we are of one accord in this. We act in love and friendship to them all, and they combine together and work for the good of each individual planet and the whole of reality, the reality of the mind.

All minds join together with the Universal Consciousness, and once you recognise the fact that you can join with us in this, even now, then you will learn so much faster what is expected of you in the future. You have linked with the Universal Consciousness, particularly when using your pendulum to help those others who have wished for information, but you have very seldom used it for yourself or your family. It has been mainly to gain knowledge for others, and perhaps for healing, but there are many ways in which the Universal Consciousness can help you, and once you have contacted this, you will find that you can derive much wisdom and pass this on to others who would like to learn more on many subjects. Much of our education is based on this Universal or Collective Consciousness, and as a result we have raised our thoughts over the centuries on to this level to gain wisdom almost instantly, by using many methods of linking together in thought. As a result, our civilisation is of one accord, we act as one, and work for the good of all.

When your planet has reached this level of consciousness, you will realise that many attitudes will be altered, and many situations will change on your planet. Those men of violence will have passed into spirit, because they are not ready to reach the fifth dimension. They will have to pass through several incarnations before they have reached this state of being. As a result, in time your planet will be like ours, one of peace, and you will have no fear of being attacked in any way. I do not mean that your part of the planet is likely to have this violence, but it has erupted from time to time in certain areas not too far from you. In your capital and various other cities, which have been bombed by certain elements, and we are very sad that this has happened to you as well as those in other countries, but this will be changed as I say, once you have passed and raised up to the fourth and fifth dimensions. These people will not be with you, and there will be a great change for the better in this respect. The children in this generation, and for generations to come will find they can accept this much easier than those of a greater age, because they have been conditioned from birth in a way that you were not, but you are readily accepting the fact that your consciousness will be altered, and you are accepting the symptoms and thoughts of how things will be in the future.

Your Earth as you know is also changing, and it will return to the state it was in before its pollution and the ravage of your beautiful forests that have been denuded, and the Earth will once more return to the state it was when man first came upon this planet, when it was green, pleasant and equable, so it will be once more, and the Earth too will raise to its higher dimension. You will see all these wonderful changes come to pass, and we, like the beings from various other planets who are helping at this time of transition, will be available to guide you on your way. I am happy to be one of those who is in contact with you now, and I hope we will have many useful communications together in the future. God bless and keep you all.

CHANNELLED COMMUNICATIONS FROM ARCTURUS ARBUL-3

Yes, we have a meeting of minds. This is Arbul, and I wish to communicate with you once more. I think that we are combining together better now, than at the beginning, I am able to lower my frequency and all is well. I realise that as yet I have not mentioned a number of things that are important to you and others. Mostly it is of those with whom we work in unity. I have mentioned that we have been raised to this higher frequency for many centuries, and it was through the Alpha Centauri beings that we were able to receive assistance, and since then we have been in constant accord with them and other beings on the fifth dimension. Also, we are in unity with the Ascended Masters of the Hierarchy, whom I mentioned in my last communication. There is a group of them, which includes the Master Jesus, Sananda, as He is known nowadays, and I also wish to mention those who work from the Angelic Hierarchy, and they too work in conjunction with the Masters.

The Archangel Michael is one of these who is very much connected with your Earth, the beloved Terra, and we hope that we can join together in this work, and connect with you and many others with whom we are in contact, in saving your Earth from any catastrophe. We do not wish anything to happen of a disastrous nature, do not worry, we have gone through this, as I have said before, and the change will be one of re-growth, a renewal and a new start in life. It is something that is completely different from anything the inhabitants of the Earth have experienced for such a long time, since the very beginning of man's time on Earth, when life was simpler.

I know that you cannot imagine how things will be, but think of yourselves as beings of light, because this is what you are. You are not aware of what you look like. You think of yourselves as beings inside your physical bodies, just as you see yourself in a mirror, and you see one another as you are, and that is how you think of yourselves, but you are great beings of light, of limitless form, and you must remember this. Try to realise that your spirituality is most important. You are your soul, and that soul has incarnated many, many times, and that soul has great experience. Some beings incarnating at present are fairly new, and have not had much experience in this way. They have perhaps more feelings of violence, and as a result, they have several incarnations to complete before they are ready to 'make the grade' so to speak, onto the fifth dimension. Therefore, they will have to wait a long time before they can accomplish this leap into a new state of being.

We are aware of what we are, because we reached that stage so long ago, but our capabilities are different from your own. We are not saying we are any better, we are just a little further along the path of experience than yourselves, and this is why we are attempting to give assistance where we can. Our telepathic abilities are such that we can communicate across space, and we have been learning to extend this capability of recent years. We have been helped in this by other beings of light, and we are always attempting to learn more. We are connected in this way with other planets, and we hope that in time your planet will also interconnect with all these other fifth dimensional planets, so that you and others upon the Earth will be able to instantly learn a great deal of information about other beings of light. Through this network of communication, great knowledge can be passed on; it is through this that we have built up our system of communication. We have improved on what we had before our new developments, so that now we can use light frequencies in order to transmit our messages.

Once you have raised your consciousness onto this higher level, this higher frequency of light, then your capabilities will be much greater. Your vibratory level will stay constant, and not be brought down by other lower frequencies. You may find when you meditate or try to use your telepathic abilities, that sometimes you find it more difficult than others; this is because you have not yet reached the capability of using light. It is a much higher frequency, but it keeps you on a constant high wave band, shall we call it, so that you are never frustrated by your capabilities, and are always able to maintain that peace and stillness from within. Sometimes you are close to this, but it is difficult to always maintain that constant capability. You will find in due course that all of you will be able to reach upto this level, and at present you are finding that you can perhaps reach this level more often than you did when you first began to meditate. It only takes practice, and also that capability of using light for this work.

The light that we use is from the Central Spiritual Sun, and that is a great body of light, which is absorbing many planets. It is difficult for us to describe it to you, but in time to come, the Earth too will be a part of these planets who are five dimensional, and using this liquid light for both communication and nourishment. You cannot yet conceive how this can be, and we cannot really describe it to you at this stage. Just accept the fact that all who are on this level of being are capable of reaching towards the Central Sun and using its power to satisfy the needs of our planet, our spacecraft, and our bodies. Everything derives power from the great Central Sun, and I know that in time to come, you too will understand and use it. Suffice to say that we will help you to gradually understand what it is all about.

As we move through space from time to time, we need to be revivified, and we have a room on board in which we have rest and absorb nourishment, and this nourishment of light is used for each one of us periodically. This light is used on Arcturus, and as I said, many planets. All of us are working for the good of the whole of our civilisation, we look up to our Elder Brethren, who help us to plan the work that we do of one accord, and is given to us when we board our spacecraft, and we travel through space having assumed command. We spend much time in travelling towards other three dimensional planets, and as we need nourishment periodically, this room in which we rest is an important one. It does not take long, because once we have assumed our restful posture, and received this liquid light, and drink the liquid, which is given to us by those within the room who look after us, we find that this revives us, and within a very short space of time we continue with the work we have committed ourselves to do.

All of us are part of a team, and the craft that we travel in is one that is designated for working with the Earth and other three dimensional planets. We have many long journeys, and leave many loved ones behind for quite some time, and although our rate of speed is extremely fast, we have great distances to travel, as you must realise, but we enjoy the work that we do. I have just assumed this work quite recently, and am learning quite fast how to control the frequency of my thoughts as I have said, and now feel that I am capable of reaching to you in a more normal manner.

Unlike Oron who is a Siriun, I am of a different size. He was speaking to you and describing the Siriun type of build. Although like them, we are quite slender, they are nearly twice our height. I would say that they are about seven feet tall, taller than most of mankind, and more slender. We are about three to four feet in size, and are also slender. Most of the fifth dimensional beings are of this type, because we do not need much sustenance. We do not need so much space around us in our ships. The ships are of a different size from the Siriuns, and there are a number of us who travel together in them, and our crew is usually about a dozen. It varies from time to time, as it depends on the size of the ship, but we travel in great comfort.

We are now stationed directly above where you live, and although you could not see our craft because it is cloaked and invisible to the human eye, obviously once you are on the fifth dimension you will see us, perhaps before then you'll see us as we really are. I am sure you would be delighted to see both the craft, and ourselves and I wish we could show ourselves now. Perhaps in time you will develop that clairvoyant ability, and the veil will be lifted, so you can both see and hear us, but we are happy to be in communication in this way at present, and hope to help you and describe how things are with us, and how they will be with you in the future. In the meantime, I give you my greetings, and my blessings to you all. Arbul.

CHANNELLED COMMUNICATIONS FROM ARCTURUS ARBUL-4

I give you my greetings from the realms of light, and I trust that in time to come you too will be able to join my companions and I upon our dimension. You cannot imagine how different conditions will be once the Earth has risen in her majesty, and you have risen to this dimension of light frequency, the fifth dimension. You can trust those who contact you from the realms of light, you can put all your faith in our guidance, because we, the Arcturians are here for the benefit of Earth dwellers. The Arcturians are some of the highest beings upon our dimension, and we have been chosen to help and guide you in the near future. There have been many in the past, who have been here within the Earth's gravity, and surrounding the planet further afield, helping to raise the consciousness of those on Earth. The time has now come when the Arcturians have to guide you in more detail. What we have to do at this time is to give more instruction upon your change in dimension, you know we have been on the fifth dimension for many centuries, and we hope we can give you the benefit of our advice.

The ship that I travel on is comparatively small, compared with many that are travelling to the Earth presently. There are some that are like luxurious hotels upon your planet, very large, with many rooms of different kinds, but they are rather like mother ships, and in this respect our ship is small, and yet adequate. Periodically we travel to the mother ships to receive instructions, and receive stocks of various supplies, but our instructions can be given to a certain extent through the mind within space. More detailed instructions have to be given face to face, so to speak; therefore, we do meet up with many of our fellow compatriots. You are living more separate lives in your own homes, so you are individualised in compartments, whereas we are used to living with groups of other beings like ourselves. It is rather like life, once you have returned to the Earth to reincarnate, you have left your fellow beings in spirit within the Universal Consciousness, and when you descend into material existence, you are separated from them. You are no longer a part of the whole, and occasionally through your life I think that some of you have experienced a feeling of loss at certain times.

Can I explain further, perhaps you have come to a certain part of the world that is very beautiful, and you feel at one with it, and yet not part of it. You feel you would love to be part of the whole, and yet you are separate. It is a longing that is difficult to describe, and can sometimes make you feel rather sad, even though you are thrilled by the majesty and beauty of your surroundings. It may be that you look into the night sky and see the stars twinkling above, and again have a longing that you cannot understand, but it is something that is deep within you. Your soul knows, and yet you are a separate being, your lower self cannot understand the feeling of longing. Perhaps you may have lived on one of those stars, another planet at sometime preceding this incarnation, and you may have a twin soul on that planet. That is almost like leaving the other half of you behind, but you cannot know this unless you have discovered it through meditation or another being communing with you. Each one of you has a twin soul either incarnating at the same time as you upon the Earth, or incarnating elsewhere, or living on another dimension. You may discover this during your lifetime or not, but it is interesting and you will find that once you have met and discovered that twin soul, in time to come you will be as one again. Probably on the fifth dimension, because there is not much time to find that soul upon the third dimension in your lives now, unless you are very fortunate. It matters not, but it may interest to you to know this fact.

At present there is a great expansion of consciousness, and you may not appreciate this, but there is a new acceleration within your lives, bringing about the changes gradually to your bodies, and to the Earth. It may be rather difficult for you to understand, but energies are being sent down to you from the Ascended Masters and many beings in the realms of light, so that gradually there are subtle changes occurring around you and within you, and you are being made aware of these changes within your lifestyle more quickly now. There will be many channelled teachings given over the next few years. You will find that there are more books on New Age subjects that are touching on this new thought and truth, which is important to all of you. I know that there are many millions who are not aware of this, and would not understand if they were made aware of it. They would think you needed to be taken away and treated for problems within your mind! I know there are such hospitals fro treatment, but you and I know that truth is often stranger than fiction, and what I am speaking about is truth, as you know, and all will know it in the future.

It is necessary to pass on this information to as many people as will accept it, because change is all around you, and the energies being sent down to accelerate this change are quite powerful. In the last communication, I mentioned that people have strange pains in their heads, or odd sensations of dizziness. All of this is a part of the change that is being wrought, but it is nothing to concern yourselves about. It is just something that will happen, and is gradually taking place. At times when you feel these strange effects, you should sit down and try to relax. Close your eyes, and fill yourselves with light. Breathe in pure light, the Christ Light that will always protect you. See yourselves filled from your toes to the top of your head with that light. This too can help you in meditation when you are attempting to raise your consciousness to hear that still small voice or any being who wishes to communicate with you, or to see clairvoyantly. If you cannot hear, you can often see symbols or colours, which can raise you to a higher state of being. All this will help you to return to your normal self, so that you are clear of any dizziness or head pains.

Filling yourself with light can always make you feel much better in yourself, linking with the Universal Consciousness, which is the consciousness that we work upon, and we link with that constantly in order to fulfil our purpose which is to serve all. We serve and help one another on our way through life, trying to reach a higher level of evolution. Even on the fifth dimension, we are attempting to rise up to the sixth dimension in time. So it is with all beings of light, as you are children of the light. We see you as children, perhaps, not in a condescending way, but in a protective way to help you in your journey to join us upon our dimension. Our task is to serve both the Masters of the Hierarchy, and God, and all whom we have promised to protect and guide. This is yourselves, the dwellers of the Earth, that beautiful planet which shines forth in the night sky. It is a planet to be proud of, and we know that now and in future days, mankind is attempting to protect it more, and restore it to what it was before it became polluted.

We cannot blame you, and we know you individually are not to blame. It is just a generality, speaking of mankind. It is mostly those who work in industry who have thoughtlessly caused this pollution, but now you are all learning to protect the rivers and oceans, and do your utmost to make conditions more as they were in the past, when there was less industry and less population on the Earth. At present the numbers of Earth dwellers have risen until they are out of all proportion to what the Earth should contain. We hope that in time to come, they will be prevailed upon to reduce the numbers, it will be necessary for these numbers to be decreased considerably before the changes come.

There is so much to do before that time, to educate those who will be remaining upon the planet, to start a new life, and we are here to give instructions as to what will be occurring in the years to come. You and others like you who are already on the spiritual path need not concern yourselves about any disasters that will occur. You will be protected by us, and others who are also guiding you from other planets. Much instruction is to be given, and I will be here to help you, and I know that you are interested and concerned. Do not worry, I will continue in the next communication with more detail on what will be occurring in the years to come. Meantime, be of good cheer, and take delight in your beautiful surroundings, the trees and flowers that are bursting forth and showing that spring is with you. It is the beginning of a new season of growth.

I give you my blessing this night, and salute you all. Arbul.

CHANNELLED COMMUNICATIONS FROM ARCTURUS ARBUL-5

All is very well. You are now on the same colour frequency as myself, that colour you call magenta, which is a reddish violet shade, and which you feel is highly sensitive. I know that when you see that colour you feel that you have reached a higher vibratory level. This is so, and it is one on which we bring energy to ourselves. It is strange, because all you knew was that when you meditated well, it was on days when you saw this colour, and therefore presumed it must be on a higher frequency. Sometimes intuition is completely correct, because this is so. We Arcturians from the fifth dimension use this colour all the time. It is one that is essential to us, and our energy is derived from such colours, including that liquid light that energises and nourishes us. We do not eat food substances such as you do on the Earth, we absorb energies and liquid light is one such energy.

I know you cannot visualise this at present, but in time you will, because your bodies are gradually altering. It is a slow process, but you will find in time that you will not feel the need for food. It takes a while before this happens fully, and it has occurred on many planets such as your own, when moving out of the third and into the fifth dimension. Your bodies will become less dense, and even now, many of you do not desire meat or any heavy foods that contain white flour and other substances such as a large amount of sugar. It is a gradual change in the habits of eating, and you will all find that gradually you will desire less food. I do not mean that at present you are over-eating, it is only that your body still needs nourishment, and it is a habit that you have always known. Your body is like a well-oiled machine, such as a car that needs petrol for it to maintain its locomotion. Without the fuel, it would stop and refuse to move. This is rather like your bodies, which require food to give you energy, so you can be active. It is mostly those who are inactive, who at present do not need so much nourishment, but eventually all of you will find that the desire for much food will decrease.

Everything is changing, including the Earth herself. You may have noticed, I am sure you have, that there were constant gales battering you over the last few months, and even the last few years there have been more powerful winds surrounding the Earth, causing disruption of many kinds. There have been tidal waves, and quite a number of buildings and bridges have been affected by these gales, causing great damage at times. It is something that strangely has occurred since your Harmonic Convergence, I think that was the name given to the time in 1987. That is the date when there was a special coming together of those of like mind, who were scattered throughout the Earth, working towards the evolvement of your species. Light workers who were aware, or had been informed of the importance of that time, and who rose at dawn to bring in the most powerful energies known on Earth for many generations. Some were aware of these energies at the time, and saw various things, such as red spiral energy being poured into the Earth, and other colours that could be seen at the time, or they just had the feeling there was an alteration in the very air surrounding you.

Some were completely unaware of anything, and this is quite understandable. Not everybody is capable of being constantly aware of everything that is happening around them, particularly if it is unseen to normal eyes, and unheard by normal ears and perception, nevertheless there was a change in the Earth and its surroundings. It was not long after that, there was an unheard of event in Britain like a tornado, which flattened trees in the south of the country in very large numbers, and affected a great number of buildings, and trees throughout the whole country, as you know. That was an event, which showed there had been a change in the climate that has continued since then, and we are aware the Earth is gradually altering its atmosphere and its very nature. You may not be aware of it, or possibly may sense a slight alteration in the air that is surrounding your part of the Earth, and which affects you and your neighbours.

It is something that is personal and some can perceive a difference, others not, it does not matter, it is happening and you and others besides you will have noticed slight differences in feelings in parts of your body, such as headaches, strange dizziness or eye movements feeling rather painful. It is all rather subtle, and can be unnoticed for some time. Sometimes the crown chakra can be stimulated quite frequently, so you are aware that you are being signalled to, from either your guide or other beings. It is a usual method, the stimulation of the crown chakra to attract the attention of one who is normally aware of this, but others may have felt this, and wondered what the feeling was. They may have felt that someone was brushing the top of their head, or if they were not in contact with any of the Higher Beings, they may feel perhaps their blood pressure had become too high and visit their doctor. Nevertheless, all these changes are occurring, but do not concern yourselves unduly, just be ready to accept it for what it is, an alteration in dimension.

The time will come when you must be prepared to help others who are not aware of what is going to happen in future days. They will all have heard from their Bible in the past of the latter days of mankind, and perhaps they do not realise that they have now come to the latter days, when changes would occur. There will be a new Heaven and a new Earth, as was foretold, and this is so, because the new Heaven is the fifth dimension, and the new Earth, is the Earth moving upwards into the fifth dimension also, and this is all part of God's plan for mankind. As He planned for the beings on other worlds, so it was planned for mankind to be ready when the latter days came, and to be forewarned that changes would be occurring both within and without. Through the mind you can be told many things, all that has been written in this communication is through the mind, and it means that your mind can link with other beings quite easily, if you will but train yourselves to listen for us.

We are here to help you, we the Arcturians are in the forefront of guiding you into the fifth dimension. Our civilisation moved upwards long ago, but we try to help all who are in a state of preparedness, and are on the brink of something new. Other beings from planets who are also on the fifth dimension, such as the Siriuns, have also been in touch with you, and there are beings from Alpha Centauri and the Pleiades amongst others, who are only too happy to do what they can to assist. Try to raise your consciousness in meditation to as high a level as you can, and know that your guides and us will help in every way. In the future we will be here to bring our ships close to the Earth, so that when there may be a time of danger for you, we can take you on board, and remove you to a safe place for the time being. It is only if this is necessary that we will do so, because we hope that you will be able to stay where you are on your planet. We are watchful always, and will continue to be so when the changes occur. It is only if there is real danger for you that this will happen.

Before that time of change, we are just trying to keep in touch with as many of you as we can, so you can tell others what will be occurring. Only those who would understand can be told that changes will be happening to people's bodies, and to the Earth. Certain parts of the Earth will be mostly unaffected by change. By this I mean there will be no danger involved for those inhabitants of that area. It is only when we feel that it is advisable to be removed to a safe place for a short while that we will interfere in any way. Be assured that conditions will be perfect for you, and we will keep you informed of what will be happening at that time. There are many spacecraft ranged around the Earth at intervals. We are in a state of readiness, but this does not mean that change is imminent. We have been here on and off for quite some time, and although I personally have only been in this vicinity for recent months of your Earth year, others have been here for many years. The time is getting near when you should start readying yourselves for change of varying kinds. Do not be alarmed in any way, but perhaps it may be as well to keep a store of food and every day household articles. I know you will not require so much food in the future, as you have in the past, but a certain amount of dried fruit, tins and packets can be easily stored.

Do not worry too much about storing water, because you will find that you can manage in time to come. You can have cartons of juices, and other liquids, but ensure they can be of use sometime ahead. If you were taken on board our ships, you would be returned safe and sound to your homes after a short space of time. We hope this will be unnecessary, and you will just remain where you are. In the meantime, keep faith, have trust, and know that all will be well, and that you will be ready when the time comes, with our help and reassurance, and the knowledge that you will not be alone. We will be here, and also others to assist you in any way we can. God bless and keep you. Arbul.

CHANNELLED COMMUNICATIONS FROM ARCTURUS ARBUL-6

My greetings to you, dear friend in the light. It is Arbul. Our spacecraft is stationed directly above your house in the fifth dimension, of course, and one day within the next few years you will be able to see it with your fifth dimensional eyes. I am promising that by the time you have moved into the fifth dimension, you will be capable of seeing us and our craft, and the craft of other beings who are here to assist and guide all on the beloved Earth.

You are presently reading a book that you have been wondering about, as to whether it is complete truth. I know that certain people believe everything they see in print, but I do not think that any who will read these communications will believe absolutely every word that they read. I am not meaning that the communications are not the truth, they are, but certain books have grains of truth within them. Always, channelled teachings are coloured by those who bring through the words. This is only understandable, because very few people can put themselves into a complete trance, and bring through communications. Most people like you, prefer to be in complete command, and just use telepathy to channel our thoughts. There is truth within everything that you read, but not necessarily complete truth.

The book you are reading, 'The Crystal Stair' has within it a large amount of truth, some of which you can accept, and other parts reject, if you feel it is not right for you. This is how it should be with all of you, accepting what you can, and I know that within that book there has been mention of all earth dwellers being uplifted both into the fifth dimension, and lifted into space craft when the changes of the Earth are imminent. Both Oron and myself have been telling you that we will be here to help you if necessary. We have given warnings and suggestions to you, so you will be ready to accept anything when the Earth changes occur, and I think as a result of this, and through reading this recent book, you are now ready to accept the fact that perhaps you will be transported from the Earth for a short while, particularly if the Earth moves on her axis, which could be likely.

It is not doom and gloom, and will be for the benefit of all that these changes will occur, because in time to come, you will find that once this occurs, there will be no violent people left upon the Earth. Those who have not raised their consciousness will not be accepted aboard our craft, nor would they accept a lift from us either. They are just not ready to accept anything like this, and would not understand what was happening. They will be swept aside, as will many who are not quite ready. Most people that you have come across, I am sure you have given a word here and there. A seed will be planted, and those people of good heart and mind will finally come to the truth of what is going to occur. I do not say that they will not need help, and this is where you come in, because those who are already on the spiritual path will be necessary to be around, in order to convey what is going to happen, and to prepare everyone for their journey for a short length of time.

As I have said, prepare a stock of food for a few months, and you may find you have other people staying with you, to consider. All of you have much to look forward to when you finally come to this time of great excitement and change. There may be a certain amount of radiation in the atmosphere, due mainly to nuclear power stations being disrupted, caused by Earth movements, but this will die down, and it is for this reason we felt we should warn you that you will probably need to be removed from the Earth for a little while. It has happened many times over, for countless thousands of years to other planets, who have changed to a higher frequency, and also had the axis of their planet turning. We have experienced the same situation on our planet, and other fifth dimensional planets thousands of years ago went through the same situation.

We know that this experience is one in which you as inhabitants of the Earth, will experience a great exultation when you raise your whole being to a higher frequency. Your lives will alter considerably, and we know your future looks very rosy to us. You will have accomplished a great deal in this particular lifetime. You are all experienced souls, ones who have held responsible positions in the past. In other incarnations you have worked with beings of light within a temple of some kind, and you have been part of that group to uphold the rights of men to worship as they feel they should. You have been in positions of authority over others at various times, and therefore you have chosen in this incarnation to raise to the highest level of which mankind is capable.

Master Jesus in His life rose upto the highest level without the energies that you have been given of recent years. He had to do this work Himself. He was a great being of light, and still is, and therefore was perhaps half way there before He passed into spirit. His ascension was a wonderful sight, and those who were able to see Him transmuting into light were changed forever. They were convinced he was the Son of God, and that His coming to the Earth was a miraculous occurrence, and something that should transform the hearts of men forever. His disciples were changed forever, but men's memories are short, and over the centuries man has not changed unduly. It is only those who have within them that feeling they might try to follow in His footsteps in time to come, and have within their hearts the golden flame of truth. We hope this golden flame will light you from within, and help you empower yourselves for your future life on Earth.

Mankind is destined to be a Son of God. He was made in the image of God, and all of you are capable of great things. We know that you have within you the power that we have to transform yourselves into lighted beings. You are children of light, and will become light when you raise upto the fifth dimension. Once you have reached that level, you will find that, like us, you are energised by light. The Earth herself will be like our planet Arcturus, in that from the centre of the planet you will receive energies that will sustain and nourish you. They will be beneficial to all of you in time to come. The Earth will be a part of the group of planets who are nourished and consumed by the great Central Sun. It is part of God's Plan that Earth will be part of this group, and that you as beings of light will be sustained and guided in the future, by many beings who are presently unknown to you.

You are aware of the Masters of the Hierarchy, including Sananda, who was Jesus, and there is the Master R also, and other Ascended Masters, who have been helping the dwellers of the Earth over many centuries. We are working with them, and we know you will learn so much from them, from ourselves and other celestial beings. Our minds are tuned to the Universal Mind, and we work consciously with this Cosmic Consciousness. Some of you can tune in occasionally to this level, and we know in the future, you will be guided from the Universal Mind on the fifth dimension, continuing on into higher levels of being in future times. As our minds are on a very high vibration, we respond very quickly to any communications that come to us. Our minds are extremely fast, compared with your own. We are not criticising you for this, and is because you are on the third dimension, and you have to experience a sea change in order that you and others on your planet will be able to tune into our minds, and to the Cosmic Consciousness without any problem in due course.

Once you have reached the fifth dimension, your bodies will become more amorphous and less dense. You will find you will not require food in the way you do at present, and your bodies will adjust accordingly. Perhaps like us, you will find most of you will need less clothing, because the atmosphere of the Earth will be altered, and it may be like Arcturus, a warmer place to live, particularly in this area that at present experiences cold in the wintertime. Other parts of your planet that at present are very hot will be altered as the Earth's axis changes. In time, when the Earth is on the fifth dimension, the atmosphere and temperature will be more generally temperate, with fewer extremes, so all of you will find it comfortable, and will not need heavy clothing. We do not wear heavy clothes, and we only dress so that we are neat and tidy to look at, and all dress in similar clothing so that we do not differ too much from one another, but that is mainly because our outlook is different from your own, which may eventually alter, and be less competitive than it is at present.

This competitiveness is meant that you feel you must try to achieve higher levels of capability than your companions. This is all based from when you were children, and you had to strive for high levels with your work at school, and I think most of the beings on your

Earth have this outlook. We have been brought up from early days to try to work together as a whole. Working as one, not striving to be better than others. It is all a matter of how you begin your life, and the training within a lifetime. Perhaps in time all of us will have the feeling we should try to help on another more, and to serve all in future days. I think those of you on the spiritual path are now feeling your lives should be of service, and have been thinking this way for some time. Less competitive than you were before, and trying to think of others and treat them as you would wish to be treated yourselves. This is good, and we applaud this trait within your characters. We hope this will be a new trend for all, and you will join with us in attempting to serve all who you meet.

      As I said, the future is very bright, and we know that although you may have some doubts about the future, but do not concern yourselves, because all of us from planets in the fifth dimension are helping, and ready to assist in every way. We have been doing this for long years, and will do more as time progresses. Work with us and the Masters of the Hierarchy, and you and others on this path will find great happiness and peace of mind, as each month and year goes by. We are with you, and we know that you have faith in God, and He has faith in us. God bless and keep you, and we will be with you again soon. Arbul.

CHANNELLED COMMUNICATIONS FROM ARCTURUS ARBUL-7

My greetings to you dear friend this night. I hope that we will have a meeting of minds, and that I can instruct you a little more on both ourselves, those living on Arcturus, and various other topics of interest. You have been wondering what the subject might be, and I know that you are interested, as perhaps others are, in what we look like. I have mentioned previously that we are quite small compared with earth dwellers. We are three to four feet in height, and quite slender, compared with most people on the Earth. It is difficult to think in terms of weight, because we are more or less weightless. We can lift ourselves quite easily from the ground, rather like levitation, and float, so that weight does not concern us, nevertheless, we are rather like some of your lighter children. That is an easy way of putting it. Our heads are perhaps larger than your own, rather as a child looks, and we have quite large eyes, compared with yours, but there the similarity ends.

We do not have hair, and we do not have protruding ears, we do have a method of hearing that is not very obvious. It is rather like birds have, just a hole at the side of the head, as you have, but smaller. Usually more than one, two or three small holes either side, looking rather like your telephone, the earphone end, and is rather similar to our ears, not so many holes as in your telephone, but that idea. It is not an obvious protrusion, because we hear with other parts of our head. Our heads are quite sensitive, and therefore we are able to pick up sounds around us rather than to either side. Our eyes serve to look outwards and inwards, so that they serve to help us telepathically like your third eye, which is gradually developing with most of those who are on the spiritual path. It is a similar idea, only we have two eyes like your own, but larger, and they serve as our outward eyes and our inward looking eyes also.

Our abilities for telepathy are very powerful. We use these all the time, so we do not need to converse with one another if we do not wish to. We have a different outlook from mankind in that, it sounds pompous perhaps, we do not like the sound of our own voices more than is necessary, though it is only certain people who are like this on Earth, those who wish to converse constantly, and at great length on various subjects. I have noticed that usually those who have a lot to say do not speak in depth on serious subjects, they are usually trivial matters that are often not the concern of others, but this is perhaps rather critical. We do not wish to criticise any of you, we are just interested, and through being interested, we have picked up various traits of those who live upon the Earth. We have noticed that those who think deeply do not always converse as often. Husband and wife, perhaps, who are on the same wavelength, and they do not need to converse, they are often thinking in a similar vein and do not feel the need to speak. Some people seem to think it is important to keep up a conversation, and that it is impolite to sit in silence. These are different thoughts from my own, and they interest us quite considerably.

We speak to one another through our thoughts, and we project our thoughts outwards towards other planets. We send healing and love, which we project towards the Earth dwellers as well. We love you, and we only wish to serve and help you in whatever way we can. This is part of our tradition, our culture, to be of service, as I have said on other occasions, and as we live in a community, we know it is essential to work together as one. The Elders send us forth on our various tasks, and they run our planet, rather like the governments of your world run their respective countries, so to speak. The leaders of your nations try to come together and unite in their way, so there will be peace throughout your world. In this way, the Elders of our planet work together, and there is no fear of war. We have overcome any dissention in this way, and this is wonderful for us, and we do hope in time to come, that the Earth too will be like ourselves, and have a new generation of peace forever throughout your planet.

Once you have risen onto the higher dimensions, we feel there will be a change in the outlook of man. All our lives are dedicated to working together, and raising young Arcturians to the way in which we live, so they can learn everything that we have learnt in the past, and to try to make them even better citizens than ourselves. There are groups of people who take care of the young on our planet, and they are brought up to learn our laws, and to be educated in a way different from your own children. Nevertheless, all are attempting to do their best for the young, both on your planet and our own. It is the young who will rule in time to come, and who will be sent forth to join with those of other planets, to be a part of the group who travel the universes and seek out those who need help in space, and beyond areas that we ourselves have known. As the universes expand, so we must travel even further afield to help others.

Our spacecraft are quite complex, and on entering them you would wonder what the various lights, buttons and screens are for. There is much to learn if you are to visit our vehicles, which we hope you will do in time, when you are required to leave the Earth in the future, and even before if you wish to. We hope you will be interested in the work we are doing, and that you would wish to learn more about or scheme of things. We have been learning more and more about the Earth dwellers, and I am extremely interested in your culture too. It is interesting to compare notes, and we have much to learn about you, as you have with us. Perhaps we have an advantage over you, because we can see you, whereas you are only aware that we are visiting your Earth in spacecraft sometimes seen, but very seldom. All that you the channel can do is record my thoughts, as I pass them to you, and you know at this time I come and visit your area with the spacecraft overhead. You know I will be here, and you wait for my signal, and then speak my thoughts, but apart from that you cannot know what I look like, because you still cannot see me.

I hope before very long that will be rectified, and we can meet face to face, so to speak. My wish is that all men will eventually be able to see us, so that they will get used to beings from other planets speaking to them, and being close without being fearful, because we mean well. We are aware that the public is genuinely rather reticent about seeing beings from other parts of the universe, and rather wary of being taken on board their craft, because it is known that periodically there have been sightings of spacecraft in various parts of the world, your world. People have been taken on board certain craft, and have reported this to their governments, in that they have been experimented on, or they have lost their memory, but they knew they were on a spacecraft for a while. This can have happened because there are some beings from certain planets who have had recourse to your kind. They have landed in remote parts of your Earth, and selected a few people to come on board their craft pretending they were friendly.

I do not think much harm occurred, but on the other hand, they had no right to abduct anyone against their will, to experiment on them in any way whatsoever. We are very much against anything of this kind, and if we saw it happening, we would do whatever we could to prevent it, and protect the Earth dwellers however we can. We do not use violence, but we can use rays that will stun other beings who are causing violent acts, so we could prevent this abduction of earthlings from happening. Have no fear though, because all that is in the past. Also it may have happened in America, and perhaps in Russia's remote areas, but it would never happen in Britain because we have been protecting your country and many others over the last few years, so we would detect other craft approaching before they could be able to do any damage or abduct anyone. We have no fear for these people, because they cannot harm us. We can project ourselves quickly into the next dimension, higher than their own, because we are higher beings than they are. They would not be doing this work if they were on our dimension. I will not go into detail, but in time you will find this out, and will know we act from the highest motives.

As mentioned, we are working with the Ascended Masters, and the Angelic Hierarchy, for the good of mankind and all other planets who are rising upwards to a higher level of consciousness. The planets themselves as you know are also rising, and will change in character accordingly. I have mentioned we are sustained through an energy that is given to us from the core of our planet, and from other sources that may be inexplicable to you at present, but we digest certain substances, mostly liquids that are energising, filled with an effervescent substance that sustains and uplifts us. Our metabolism is higher than your own, and we need this substance to maintain this high level of being. You will be altering, and will be able to be sustained by different substances from those you have at present. Time will tell, and I am sure that the Earth will provide whatever is required for your new appearances and needs. The Earth herself will energise from the great Central Sun, and liquid light will pour out towards the Earth and yourselves, to sustain, nourish and protect you. You cannot imagine how this will be at present, but everything will come clear eventually.

I have mentioned that we travel across the universes on our craft. I have not travelled far afield, apart from my own planet of Arcturus to the Earth. As I have said, this is a new venture for me, and therefore I have not travelled in other directions, but the distance involved between our two planets is quite considerable. There is no such thing as time, and we can transport ourselves in the twinkling of an eye from one place to another. Therefore, you cannot conceive of the speed we can travel. Your thoughts are slow compared with our own, and your deliberations about the speed of light, and speed of craft travelling from Earth to a certain point in space are completely different from our own concepts, because you are on the third dimension, and we are on the fifth, and so your thoughts are therefore different. You must reckon that the distance involved is considerable for those on the third dimension, and the necessary fuel that will project the craft from Earth to that point in space has to be worked out. However, new concepts will come, and you will realise there will be no such thing as gravity, and no great expense involved in space flight once you have moved to the higher dimension.

Everything will change, and new thoughts will come into being. We wish you well for the future, and we take great care in our presentation of new topics for you. We have great pleasure in giving you these communications, and we know you look forward to hearing from us as time progresses. God bless, Arbul.

CHANNELLED COMMUNICATIONS FROM ARCTURUS ARBUL-8

Greetings to you, dear child of the light. I am happy to speak to you. Your note is sounding higher than it did when you first tried to attune. You are on the magenta vibration, which is the colour that we are in tune with; our atmosphere is of this colour and this note. It is difficult to describe to one on three dimensions, but each colour sounds a note that some of you may be aware of, and the magenta is one of the highest. We also sound a note, all beings of light do, and this note varies from one individual to another. Those on a lower vibratory level sound a lower note on the scale, and it is hard to imagine if you cannot hear it, but to those on the fifth dimension, our note is very much higher than anything you would be able to hear. Like animals who can tune into notes on a whistle, which does not register a sound to human ears, but to a dog it sounds very tuneful, and it registers on their auditory level, as opposed to the humans. Animals are able to tune into levels which humans cannot hear, rather like when a storm is approaching, or earthquake is about to occur, the animals are aware at least half an hour before any human can be aware of any danger approaching.

I wish to speak about levels of consciousness, and I hope in time to come that humanity will have raised his level of consciousness so that all will be able to tune into our vibratory level. I am sure once you are on the fifth dimension you will see us, but we hope you will see, hear and sense us before you raise onto the fifth dimension. We are very much aware that there is a great deal of work to be done before this happens, and increasingly more people will be learning to meditate regularly. This is the only way, practice makes perfect, and sometimes your meditations may not be successful, but if you do it twice daily, you will have attempted to raise your consciousness to that higher level, and something that cannot be rushed. There are days when it is easy, and others when you can get no response, but do not concern yourselves, as this does occur with everyone periodically, and as long as you make the effort to reach upwards and inwards to hear that still small voice, and to raise onto a higher note, then you will be rewarded, and each of you will be improving your capabilities in this direction.

We had to do this in the past, in order to improve our capabilities. We felt it was important to attune to the Cosmic Consciousness so as to be more sensitive to other beings of light, and to be capable of visualisation. This is extremely important and can help you to raise your consciousness. It means you can attune to other peoples' consciousness, even other beings who are from far distant planets. If you can attune to their consciousness you will be given a symbol, shape or a picture within your mind. If you cannot hear words, then these symbols and pictures will be very valuable to you, and if you can register these on your consciousness, it means you can commune with one another, because that being of light from another planet will be capable of registering what is on your mind very capably. Telepathy is second nature to all beings on the fifth dimension or higher, and visualisation is also important, because in being able to communicate in this manner, you will be able to communicate without words, only using thought and telepathy is what is used between all of us.

Many of us do not use the spoken word very often; it is thought that is quickly transferred from one of us to another being, in another craft, though usually through the use of telepathy we have to be reasonably close to one another. We cannot communicate vast distances through telepathy, but there are other means of transferring our thoughts to one another upon our ships. Even symbolic messages can be transmitted between ships, so we can transmit instantly using a machine that sends out symbols and pictures. We can speak into these machines like a microphone, to register onto a screen, and we can transfer our thoughts and instructions to one another this way. All fifth dimensional beings have this equipment on board their craft, and therefore we can help one another when help is required, or we can combine forces to help mankind or other beings on planets who are in a similar situation to yourselves, at the point where change is occurring, and when that time of the Earth changes comes, we will be ready.

There have been hundreds of channels who have transferred our thoughts for many years. We have attempted to reach many who are able to attune to us, and over that time we have achieved a network of those who will be open to our thoughts, a network of lightworkers who will be ready and able to transmit our messages to humanity. Perhaps in time we will reach your television screens and transmit what is necessary to be given to the people of your various lands, but time must be given for this to be accepted, and to initiate these procedures very gradually, because we do not wish to alarm anyone by appearing on your screens.

We try to keep a low profile, and do not wish to unnerve people, but it is important that word should be given to those who are leading the countries, and perhaps some of them will rise to a higher level of consciousness, and may attune to us. It will be much easier if they also can receive our messages, in order to give comfort to any who are nervous of the change that will occur. We know that leaders in eastern countries meditate regularly, as part of their religion, for they are brought up in this way from being quite young. It is only through this capability that one can develop one's spirituality and gradually the western countries are changing their outlook on this, and are accepting the benefits of being able to shut off the outer world and concentrate on that inner core of divinity that is within each one of you, waiting to be developed. It is strange how so many people can live their lives without being aware of this inner life.

We have known about these capabilities all our lives, but originally our planet of Arcturus went through this change you are beginning to go through many centuries ago, and we have only known how it is at present with everyone who inhabits our planet, being very sensitive and of a high dimension, on a higher vibratory level than is capable on your Earth. Our atmosphere is completely different from yours, and we exist in a different state of being. We do not need nourishment, and have mentioned this before. When we compare our lives with your own, we realise how much time is spent in preparing meals for nourishment of the body on the Earth. It is obviously very essential, but quite time consuming compared with our lives, and you will find a great change in your daily routine, because we derive our nourishment from our very planet, and from the great central spiritual sun, which nourishes the planet itself, and which will gradually nourish the Earth when the time comes.

Our time is spent in serving the elder brothers, and they rule our planet in a kindly way. We will have much to say on this in future times. The teachings for our young are all important, and many experienced beings are in charge of the young, who have much to learn within a short space of time, before they are able to join us in our work. There are many lessons they have to learn, which involve a high vibratory level, and certain complex codes of practice that we cannot really tell you about, because it is something that the elder brothers have evolved over the centuries, and which we will be able to teach you when you have reached our higher level of being. We look forward to this, because we live to serve, we only wish for you to reach our levels of consciousness, and then be able to pass on much knowledge to those who have still to reach it. What is necessary is a very high level of thought, so you can attune to the Cosmic Consciousness, and by doing so, you will be able to attune to our vibratory level. It will only take a short space of time, for those who can already hear us, and we hope that many of you will be able to both hear us, and attune to the Cosmic Consciousness, which all beings communicate within.

As you know, we are all one, and when you reach that transition, you will join us, and become one with us and all other beings of light in the fifth dimension. There is so much to look forward to, and the feeling of brotherly love is emanating towards you from all of us. We really look forward to you joining us in this level of love and light. There is much power within the Cosmic Consciousness that will help you when the changes come, to adapt your minds to everyone. Thought is so powerful, and once you have developed that positive thought and capability of true visualisation, then you will find it so much easier to communicate with us, and others who are from planets even further afield than Arcturus. We wish you well. Go with god and be of good cheer, because we love each one of you, and we hope to help you all in every way possible. God bless, Arbul.

CHANNELLED COMMUNICATIONS FROM ARCTURUS ARBUL-9

I, Arbul greet you this night, and we from Arcturus wish you well. You are all children of the light, those who are aware of our companionship with you. We link in love with the Universal Mind, another name for the Cosmic Consciousness, in which we all have our being. We are all one; there is no separation between beings of light and love. All planets on the fifth dimension dwell in this consciousness, and we live to serve one another, and those on Earth, and other planets like yours who need assistance periodically. This is one of those times when we know the Earth dwellers are approaching that time of transition. All of us have been through this time, and we know what it is to have this new awareness, this new energy pouring in from above, or so it seems. All of us are assisting at this time, and have been for many years, now is the time when more Earth dwellers are becoming conscious of change all around them. It seems that this upliftment of consciousness is spreading and that is what we are trying to help you with, and have been doing for so long.

It is part of our work, and the work of beings from other distant planets from Earth, such as Alpha Centauri and others, who helped us in the past, and have been helping you alongside ourselves. As said, we work under Lord Sananda, helped by the Archangel Michael, and there are so many of us working together that we cannot fail, we are all part of creation, all co-creating many worlds within worlds, which are spinning as a result of our help, and expanding the Universe in which you live, expanding to other universes that surround us. It is all so vast that you cannot comprehend its extent, we cannot be fully aware of the number of universes that continually expand and become part of all creation. Everything is becoming so vast that the minds of all beings are constantly being uplifted, so that we can try to comprehend what is occurring around us. It is a cosmic explosion of life.

As you know, life on Earth began many billions of years ago. I will not expand my thoughts on this, but you are aware of the time it has taken for the Earth to evolve to this state. Try to imagine the Earth being a grain of sand, and the other grains around it are other planets and stars within the universe, and in this way your minds can then accept how extremely small your life on Earth is, compared with God's Universes. You feel you cannot imagine the size of this universe, let alone other universes that are constantly created, so that your comprehension of infinity is rather lower than you would wish, but it is all so vast that your minds cannot take it all in. Everything dwells within the Universal Mind or Cosmic Consciousness, and so within that soup of space, shall we say, that is a rather loose term for the vastness of your universe, there are so many millions and billions of planets and stars, and upon all of them or certainly most of them, there are beings who exist in different life forms.

In the past, mankind thought that he was the only sentient being within his universe. He imagined perhaps there might be small beings living on Mars, which was the only apparent star which might be able to support life as you know it, but as you are aware, you now know there are many more evolved beings than yourselves, far more than you could ever imagine even now. As a result, mankind is still learning many of the things that beings on the fifth dimension learnt hundreds or thousands of years before, but we do not wish to make you feel small, you are just appreciating how much, or how little mankind knows. He is considerably lower on the evolutionary ladder than he imagined, but this doesn't matter, it is not important either to man or ourselves, so long as man takes his part in God's Plan, and appreciates the amount of education he still requires, both mentally and spiritually. If all of you are willing to continue this learning process, then we are very happy, because we are part of God's Plan for mankind, and many others, and we hope we can both teach you our knowledge and the wisdom that was given to us from other beings of light far in advance of ourselves, and continue with the work we have set ourselves to do in order to help Earth dwellers in their advancement.

Those of you on the spiritual path have accepted how little mankind has evolved, and are attempting to better yourselves, and to raise your consciousness to new levels of being, always striving to raise onto a new level, and be able to link your minds with any beings who are ready to help you, such as guides, angels and other beings of light. We always maintain this high level of conscientiousness, and to play our part in mankind's evolution, and other dwellers of the third dimension.

Sound is very important in helping to raise consciousness. If you can imagine the higher your note sounds, then you reach a higher vibratory level. To make a toning sound from each level of your chakras is an important learning process. Sound the note that is easiest for you, starting at the base chakra, and then proceed to sound an Om for each chakra, until you reach the crown chakra, and make the highest note that you can possibly reach. In this way, working up the seven chakras, you can raise your vibratory level gradually. Do this periodically every week or so, and you will find a difference. You will find it was easier to raise your consciousness after you sounded this Om for each chakra. Should you feel a vibration within your body, then this shows you that your capabilities have improved.

Try to pass this knowledge to others, so they can learn to sound these notes. Explain to them about the chakras, and that they are centred on the endocrine organs of the body, and can make the etheric body more active, and through meditation they can reach higher levels of consciousness. The evolvement of the soul is one of the reasons for living on Earth, and you know that through reincarnating, you are developing new capabilities that you learn to hone the soul to a brighter level of being, rather like working a piece of metal. When a sword is plunged into the fire, and is brought out red hot, honing it down to a finer point, this analogy is like your soul, working it through fire and water, the experience of all lifetimes, so that you progress to finer beings.

Remember always the spiritual nature of man is part of the ether that is all part of the whole. The ether permeates through everything that is alive, and spreading across the universe, and to further universes of which you have no knowledge. Think of your body being a part of all that, and each one of you, and all of us on other dimensions are all a part of that one ether. Our bodies of light on the etheric are all one, linking with one another through light and love, and constantly learning and experiencing through our lifetimes. It is the etheric weaving through each lifetime, and each being of light, remembering always that your link with one another is through love, and God sends forth His love to all. He is within each one of you, and He is the link that communicates His love to all, all beings of light on all stars and planets throughout the great dominion that belongs to God.

There are several of our craft from Arcturus circling the Earth at this time. All of us link together to reassure one another that we are still doing our work, and attempting to help others. We have many on board, who are extremely interested in the work that is being done, and they watch over us while you and I communicate with one another. Sometimes they send their loving thoughts through me, and they try to instil within you their thoughts that are given through me. I am still learning in order to convey the messages that I give to you. It has taken time for my thoughts to become one with yours, as I said originally, all of us work at a higher rate than yourselves. A higher vibratory rate that is rather like insects, move faster than yourselves, their buzzing sound if slowed down would change considerably, and be similar to the little people, who speed along at a very high rate, which you cannot see, and their sounds are high above what a human can hear, then you have a faint idea of our rate compared with your own, which seems laborious to us, and very heavy and slow.

But gradually I am becoming accustomed to the speed you work at. I am not criticising in any way, because we on Arcturus were on the third dimension originally, and I was not aware of this when I came onto the planet. I have learnt it since, but now you can imagine how it is rather difficult to adjust, but I am learning, and I hope that in future times I will be able to teach you more of our life on Arcturus. We wish you well, and send all of you our love and blessings this night. God bless, Arbul.

CHANNELLED COMMUNICATIONS FROM ARCTURUS ARBUL-10

Greetings to you dear fellow being of light. I know that you cannot see me, and that you would wish to see me sometime, but I communicate through the mind. Your invocation to the light is very true, and I know was given to you by the Master R. He works with many beings of light at present, and all of us throughout the realms of the fifth dimension are working with light and sending it towards you upon the Earth. As you know, the great central sun is a part of our consciousness, it is God and everything, we are all one and that oneness of which we are a part is to spread to the Earth dwellers. At present on the third dimension, so many are completely unaware they are part of everything. If they are aware of the Universal Mind, they are beginning to awaken to this fact of oneness, there is no separation, but on the third dimension it is natural to be separate. When you were born, the only oneness you knew was with your parents, and if you had brothers or sisters, one with them as a family unit. Being born on the third dimension gives a feeling of separateness, once you have left your home you feel you do not belong to any one being until you find one whom you love.

It is rather difficult as a being on the fifth dimension to explain to you how different it is for us. We have never known any separation and we do not realise until we see for ourselves how different it is for you. In time, once you have risen to the higher level, you will appreciate how we are not separate from the rest of the universe. We are all part of one great universal family, and God is part of everything, as you know, but even more so once on the fifth dimension. You will be aware of the nuances and wonderful feeling of lightness that is part of your very being. You may have dreamt of flying on the astral plane, which is part of the fourth dimension, and this feeling of freedom is wonderful to you, and when you move upwards to where we are, you will be aware of this great freedom of your soul. Your body will no longer seem heavy, and unable to move with that freedom as in a dream. It will truly become a body of light. Your spiritual nature will come to the fore, and your physical bodies will become lighter, and you will be true beings of light.

We hope our communications with you help to inspire and uplift you with the thought of how things will be in the future. We know you have to live in the now, and try not to think too far ahead. Your life has to continue as it was before, but you can learn to appreciate how you will be in the future when the changes have taken place, and the Earth is also on the fifth dimension. Those changes have been spoken of for some time, and have already begun. It all takes time, and until the more dramatic changes ensue, you can continue as usual, living your life, but always include meditation twice daily if you can, in order to link with the realms of light and attune to higher beings, or even your higher self. It is important to have this quiet time to link with the Universal Mind, of which we are a part, and you are part of it though many are not aware of this. It matters not, because there is a large percentage of Earth dwellers now on the true spiritual path, who meditate with their higher selves, or with other beings who will give them truth.

I know you sometimes wonder if it is truly a being from another planet who contacts you, and perhaps other people wonder whether this is so. It is only human to question anything that is given to you, particularly through thought, but truly I am from Arcturus. I am Arbul and am presently stationed right above this house. My craft is there, and I am within a room of this house. Truly I am from the fifth dimension, and therefore cannot be seen, except by those who are capable of this vision, very few upon planet Earth are capable of being able to see beings of this dimension. Perhaps they can see spirit beings who have recently been upon the Earth as human on the third dimension, but very few have the clairvoyance to be able to reach onto a dimension as high as the fifth. We are able to reach the sixth dimension at times, but we are permanently on the fifth, which means we can transport ourselves extremely swiftly in the blink of an eye to another part of the galaxy.

Our spacecraft are ready to move at a second's notice. We have established the art of teleportation, and use it constantly while on our home planet. Many times we transport ourselves instantly to meet up with others on other parts of the planet, but we also have smaller craft available if we wish to use them, rather like you have cars for use, and it is quite pleasant to travel on our smaller craft, for pleasure rather than work, which we are doing at present. This is something else you can visualise for future times, teleportation to transfer yourselves instantly to another part of your planet as we do, in due course. You will find others who are unaware of these future events, and will need explanations of what is occurring. You have been told this is part of your work, and others on the spiritual path will be helping to direct others, and help them in their new thinking. These are people who are not quite as far along the path as you, but who will be ready to accept these new events occurring, and will raise their vibrations sufficiently to accommodate themselves into the fifth dimension when the time is right.

We are aware that you and others who know the truth of future times are feeling you belong to some secret society that can never divulge the arcane knowledge that you have. I know it is frustrating for you at times not to be able to pass on this knowledge to your friends, who are not on the same wavelength, shall we say, and you pass the time of day with, and enjoy their company, but cannot share this important secret with them. At times you are tempted to tell them, and you passed a little seed of knowledge to see if it would be planted in fertile ground, and receive feedback of this knowledge that you have and long to give to them, but you realise these little seeds have been scattered to not avail, and therefore you cannot tell them more. They are not ready to accept this knowledge, however, perhaps in time they will learn more. You have occasionally lent books that have hidden meanings, part real truth of which you are aware, and part fiction of which they are aware, and sometimes it helps to reveal real truth to them, and they may dwell on this, and perhaps ask you questions in the future.

You know the books that you have passed on to others, and I am aware of this Beryl, hoping they will talk about and discuss things with you, about the future and about life after life. Sometimes they will accept this, but many times it is just a waste of time, and you cannot really do much more than hint about the knowledge you have of other planets and life upon them, and how things will be in the future here. You will be able to many miraculous things when the faith is there to do them. Healing can be done through the power of prayer, and the power of channelling pure healing light to others, and it could be viewed as miraculous. Healing can take place at many levels, and subconscious levels of understanding stored there can be brought into the conscious mind when an individual is ready, and it is hoped that it will occur.

We are consciously working with light constantly, attempting to bring light to the world of men, to enlighten their minds, and lighten their bodies and thoughts. Light and love are all powerful, as you know, as in your Great Invocation, it is an extremely powerful prayer, bringing light and love into the world of men, as we are attempting to do, working with the Masters of the Hierarchy. All will come to pass. Just have faith and we will continue with our communications in the future. God bless and keep you all. Arbul.

CHANNELLED COMMUNICATIONS FROM ARCTURUS ARBUL-11

Greetings to you, fellow beings of light. I am here from Arcturus; it is Arbul who speaks, happy to be in communication once more. All those on my spacecraft are interested in the work we do, and are listening in to our communication. We have many craft that visit the Earth, and over the last few years there has been heightened interest in the channellings that have been achieved. We are pleased we have managed to cause this interest on Earth, and we hope to continue to create more channels of light who will bring through our thoughts to all who will be helped by us in the future. We know beings from other planets have been helping to bring through communications over many years, and all of us are to be here to help when the transition time comes. Once Earth has raised into the fifth dimension, and all of you who live here who are on the spiritual path of awareness, will be joining us on this new dimension. You are gradually raising your consciousness so you can link with us, and we know there are many who are interested to hear of any new developments.

All who work from our ship are constantly in communication with our home planet Arcturus, and those who link with us on the planet bring us news. We have always felt a certain home sickness when we are away from home, and we always wish for news from those whom we love. We are not as you are, in individual houses, we live in community with others, and work together for the good of the whole, and we know that in time to come, you too will link together in groups more than you do at present. There will be changes in thought, and all who think in the same way as those who read this, and are on the spiritual path, will realise there is no separation and all are one. You are aware that all beings should think as one, and those who are in confrontation with one another on the Earth will gradually appear to change their way of thinking and will 'back off', so there is no violence, or anger, and people will join together in love and compassion for one another as those on our planet have been acting towards one another for so many centuries. You are rather like children to us, we are not talking to you in a condescending manner by any means, but we recognise the fact you are still learning to cope with one another and be more in tune. Many planets have experienced what you are experiencing, and have been doing so for many centuries. We recognise this, and know we had gone through these phases and risen above them, and learnt how it is to consider others as we do ourselves. This is what we and everyone have been working for, the Masters and those who serve them, for so long, to bring about a complete change in man's outlook.

The change must come soon, and we know many of you have been trying to send out love and light for many years, towards those places on the Earth that need light shone upon them. We recognise this and salute you for the work you have been attempting to do. We realise mankind is beginning to alter his ways very subtly, and the fact that many are attempting to heal the Earth herself, to restore the balance of nature, and this is essential, so the changes that will come about will not be too violent. You realise there will be changes that have to come about before you move into a higher dimension, but if man can alter his way of thinking, and raise his consciousness, then the changes will be less extreme. All of us are working to this end, and my fellow beings of light and I are happy to be a part of this team of light workers. You are in a network of light workers like ourselves, and we are coming together in thought in this way, to try to raise and lighten the consciousness of all. It is all part of God's Plan for mankind, and we from Arcturus are a part of that small band of beings who wish to help.

There are beings of all shapes and sizes who are taking part in this great exchange of consciousness. We hope that those of us from Arcturus will find our way in encompassing the Earth in light and healing. We have been working our way around the Earth, contacting various channels, and we know you are grateful to us and to the other beings from the Pleiades, Sirius, Reticulum and other planets of which there are too many to mention, but you know all of us are on your side, working for the good of the whole. The Arcturians have been doing this for so long, we find it a simple matter to extend this work to another planet. We have been always working for one another, and returning to the home planet and Elders for whom we work. From time to time, people have seen our craft that encircle the Earth. Many are not able to attune sufficiently to see us, but some have seen us, but mostly we cloak our craft to be invisible, so that we do not cause any problems. We do not wish people to rush about in horror thinking the planet is being attacked! We only wish to come close so we can beam down towards you in order to communicate.

Many of your television programmes in the past have shown beings from planets, as being very strange and sometimes hostile, but certain programmes have shown that there are benign beings, and most of us who work towards the benefit of the Earth have been protecting all of you from any danger. We are always present, and most places on the Earth are protected from those who may not be friendly. There are occasional beings who are not of the light, but we protect you from these darker beings, and know that all in your country are protected permanently. All members of your society are being protected from any intruders from the dark planets. We cannot protect you from violent members of your society, but we can certainly protect you from other space people.

Gradually the Earth is moving upwards, slowly but surely, onto this new dimension that we exist on. You will find you can see clairvoyantly, which you could not do before. You will find you will improve in your attunement to your guide or other beings of light who wish to communicate with you. You will find that all of you will be channels, and is quite simple to attune to other beings on other dimensions if you have the faith and confidence to know that if your thoughts are pushed to one side, and you have said a prayer, you can attune. You will find this easier as time progresses, I promise you this, and all of you will be able to gradually be in communication with more and more beings of light. You will find out who they are, you will challenge them, because you should always ask if they are of the Christ Consciousness, and if so, all will be well, and you will have true communications that will be of great interest to you in future times. All of you will be able to reach higher than you can at present, and we will guide you in your lives, attempting to help you through the transition time.

Therefore, instead of meditating morning and night, you will find you can attune at any time. Your life will be a true meditation even though you are living on a physical world; you will find your link with the realms above will be simple. The veil will thin and you will find great happiness and pleasure in communication with many beings who will make themselves known to you. All of us are attempting to communicate with you and be of help at this time of change, and that is our true purpose in life at present. So please be happy to join with us in this work. We will keep in touch and communicate constantly with you in the future. In the meantime, I give you my blessing this night, and may God be with you always, Arbul.

CHANNELLED COMMUNICATIONS FROM ARCTURUS
ARBUL-12

This is Arbul; I give you my greeting this night, and wish to speak to you on many things in this last communication. I have not said previously whether we are part of Ashtar Command like Oron of Sirius. This is partly because, we and several other spacecraft from Arcturus have not yet reached the status of Ashtar, but we hope to join him very soon. Many of our craft are a part of the Command, and we are also training for that purpose. It is something all of us hope to do, to reach to the level of the Ashtar Command. There are many beings from different planets who join together to work for the good of the whole, with many beings of light, guiding and directing the work we do.

As you know, the Masters of the Hierarchy are part of the number of light beings and the highest of them, and members of the Angelic Hierarchy such as Michael also link with beings from planets far and wide. He works for the good of mankind, and is closely connected with the Earth, as you know. For millennia he has worked for mankind and beings on other planets, of which you know not, but he is a wonderful being of light and has great power, wielding the sword of light for the good of all, and he is at the right hand of Sananda, or Jesus, who has incarnated upon the Earth several times under different names. He has incarnated on Venus, and also briefly on Arcturus. This is why we are full of enthusiasm to work under Sananda and Ashtar.

When I first spoke to you and mentioned Arcturus, you had not heard of it, and had to search for it in a book for quite a while. Perhaps this is good, as it means you have no preconceived ideas about Arcturus. You did not know of its existence, and discovered it was a bright star in the Bootes constellation. I know you recognise this fact, and now realise that even though it appears to be only a star, and you were not aware that beings could live on stars. Mankind always expects beings to live on larger planets, such as Mars or Saturn. You could not imagine they could survive on a star like Arcturus, Sirius, or the Pleiades. All of these are inhabited by beings who are very far advanced, compared with Earth dwellers, but many things can be misunderstood if you do not have the knowledge. It is rather like science, if you are not aware of facts, you think they do not exist. It is purely a question of learning about things, and putting them first and foremost in your mind. The facts are important, and you find sometimes that truth is stranger than fiction. The fact is that we do exist, and have existed for millennia before the Earth was inhabited.

Therefore, consider how much has been learnt in that time, and also consider time, because it is something that is continuous, and if we in another dimension existed long before the Earth and those upon it existed, consider also that time being man-made is non-existent in our own dimension, the fifth, or higher ones, and consider then that in all that 'time' we have been learning so many things, technological discoveries, and that which governs the spirit and mind. There are many parts to a being, not just the physical, but mental and spiritual sides that continue forever and never fade, they never die. Therefore, all parts of the whole are important, so what you should concentrate on is not necessarily just the physical body, but also the spiritual side, which is always constant. Our star, Arcturus, holds many beings of light, we are an old and ancient civilisation compared with yours, therefore, think of us as being full of wisdom and experience, and we can help to guide you on your way. Do not consider us superior, because we do not wish to convey that within your thoughts, we only wish to help. We have been guarding many secrets over the millennia, secrets of how to live one's life to the full.

We have a different method of living compared with those on the Earth. We live in large groups, and continually help to improve each other's capabilities in many ways. Once our companions have reached a certain level of being, we hope to guide them if we are older or more experienced than them. We constantly help and encourage them to improve, and become more experienced and better in many ways than they have been. Perhaps this is unclear to you, but we are constantly working our way up the ladder, not of success, but of achievements. So we are always striving to improve in every way, climbing up that ladder of spirituality, and teaching those who need help that has been given to us, handed down to us from the Elders of our community. They have always had high ideals, and through enlightenment, we have learned to be entirely public spirited, you might say on Earth. At any rate, we are taught from a very early age to develop capabilities that on Earth are not possible yet, but in time, you too will be able to reach to even higher levels of spirituality than those which you are attempting to achieve presently through meditation. This is something we are taught from a stage like Primary School upwards.

It is not a matter of schools here, but groups of beings of light. Rather like your nursery schools, for instance, which are small groups of children, not very many at a time, but who are banded together to be given assistance and guidance gently, and in time to come those little people go to school, and our young ones are guided in this same way, gradually but firmly raised to higher levels, learning all the time. High standards are set here on Arcturus, and as time progresses, each group is segregated into specialist groups at the place of learning, and from time to time, different members of the society help to give them education in many subjects. This learning continues, and groups of us help throughout the years to give guidance and security, but life is completely different here than on the Earth, and with being in the fifth dimension, our needs are few, and so the learning process continues more constantly than upon Earth, with fewer intervals, because little time is needed for energy here. It is a different method of nourishment required upon Arcturus. We breathe in light, and great power from our planet, which provides us with sustenance, rather like manna from heaven, which was given to those Biblical characters who needed help, and were given this nourishment when nothing was available for them.

I know there are many things you would wish to know, and perhaps in the next series of communications you may be able to find out more, but in the meantime, I hope you will bear with me in the fact that I wish to talk on other subjects today, as well as Arcturus. You know we are stationed above the house and that I have come down on a beam of light into your room, so I can speak to you through your mind, and be constantly with you while you receive my thoughts. It is in this way I can learn how it is that your mind can accept these thoughts. Our minds have been working in this way constantly. We do not require speech as such, and therefore it is interesting for me to see how your mind and speech centre work together. As we watch those on Earth, and try to study how you live and function, it is of great interest to us to try to work out how we can help you when the time of transition comes.

You are aware there have been other beings in the past who have watched the Earthlings, and have abducted them periodically. These have not been Arcturians or those of the Ashtar Command. They have been members of other planets that have had no conscience, and have experimented in the past on humanity. They did not really wish to hurt anyone, but have caused concern and fear of spacecraft, and therefore we usually try to cloak our craft, so they are invisible. We recognise that Earth dwellers have been used to a certain extent by these unscrupulous beings, and we hope you will understand this will not occur again. This is one reason why the Ashtar Command was formed, to protect humanity, and we hope this fear has gradually diminished over the years that have intervened. It is perhaps forty years or more since these happenings occurred, and we have seen to it that they will not happen again. Over these years, you have been protected, and we observe humanity and contemplate the various functions of your bodies. We recognise that you need nourishment at present, but in the future, once you have raised into the fourth and fifth dimensions, this will become unnecessary, and therefore your bodies will take on a different look.

You will gradually become more amorphous like us, and at that time your molecular structure will be able to pass through walls and floors, and as a result, you will be as we are, but this will be a gradual process. Do not think you can suddenly walk through a door without opening it, because I think you will be rather dismayed and have a sore head. Remember it takes time for this to occur; so do not expect the change to happen at once, it will not! Just accept it will happen, and those people who have seen beings from spacecraft, have recognised that they passed through walls and suddenly appeared in a room. For they are from another dimension, and much is self-explanatory when you are on the same dimension as us. This is why people have seen a spacecraft take off and disappear; they have gone from the third to fifth dimensions. It may be rather unnerving for those who have seen this, but most people accept we can control our craft much better than the three dimensional craft you have, and is due to the fuel intake, and our craft are propelled differently.

It is impossible to explain how our craft are manoeuvred, just accept we can do much that you will do in future times with your spacecraft. At present, it needs a great deal of propulsion to reach out to overcome the Earth's gravity, and enter into space, as you call it. We appreciate many things you have achieved in the time you have accomplished them. Men landing on the moon, and achieving new technology in the space of a few decades, but within the next few decades many more things will be achieved than you could ever imagine in your wildest dreams.

Now I must say farewell, as time is short, I will contact you again before too long. Meantime, God's blessing be upon you all this night.
Arbul.

CHANNELLED COMMUNICATIONS FROM SIRIUS, ARCTURUS, PLEIADES, & BETELGEUSE

SECTION THREE
PLEIADES

CHANNELLED COMMUNICATIONS FROM THE PLEIADES
Book Three

CONTENTS	Page
Section 1 – Caristal	93
Section 2 – Caristal	96
Section 3 – Caristal	99
Section 4 – Caristal	102
Section 5 – Caristal	105
Section 6 – Caristal	109
Section 7 – Caristal	112
Section 8 – Caristal	116
Section 9 – Caristal	120
Section 10 – Caristal	123
Section 11 – Caristal	126
Section 12 – Caristal	128

Channelled by Beryl Charnley

CHANNELLED COMMUNICATIONS FROM PLEIADES CARISTAL-1

It is now time to speak to you, Beryl, this is Caristal. You have brought down the violet fire in a vortex. This is good, it helps to unite our minds together, and I hope I can tell you all that I wish to today. This is a new experiment for us and it is early days, as previously I have just made myself known to you, and you have written down my thoughts given to you in an earlier meditation. We have to adjust our minds to one another, and I know you have found it difficult recently to link with the realms of light, having been away from home, but now we are adjusting together and I will proceed. I am hoping that during our links together through our minds, I will be able to give you some help and knowledge from our world.

We from the Pleiades have been in contact with humanity for many centuries. Although it was not known until recently, we have contacted people occasionally on the Earth. In the early days, these things were kept as arcane knowledge, so it was not widely known, but it has been revealed to humanity that we have been contacting the Earth for some time. It is only of recent years that all this knowledge has come to light, that beings from space as you call it, from other worlds, have been communicating with humanity, and attempting to spread wisdom. We are a highly evolved species, and we have been spreading our wings, shall we say, throughout the universe in our ships, for longer than I could tell you. It is part of our heritage, space travel as you call it, and is just part of our life, and has always been so. It is part of our daily experience that our people come and go, as you alight from planes on your world, our people alight from spaceships, and we can travel through thought. We have always done so, as far as I can remember.

Thought travel or teleportation will come to you in time, once you have all achieved that transition into a higher dimension, which is to come in a short while. Gradually, mankind is changing his ways of thought. More are open to the idea that others are more advanced than humanity. It is strange is it not, that mankind has always thought that he was the only being alive throughout the whole of the universe? There had been suggestions that there were men from Mars, the little green men, which was the only thought on the subject, and everywhere else throughout the universe was dismissed as being totally impossible for life to exist other than on Earth! I suppose it is just that mankind was not ready to accept any other being who was capable of living as man has done over the years, and experiencing many changes throughout the last hundred years, for instance, when so many inventions came about, like plane flight and others previous to that. Machines were constructed that had not been conceived of before, and great discoveries made that were to change man's life, simple things like the telephone, cars, and complex machinery, electronics, technology, everything that has been created over the last century.

All these had been discovered way back in time on our planet, and many others. All this was simple, compared with our technology, but there again, comparisons are odious are they not, and we hope that gradually our two worlds will unite, and be able to communicate with one another, and perhaps man will be able to travel to our planets, and many others who have been linking with mankind like the Siriuns, beings from Orion and Alpha Centauri, also many other planets that have attempted to communicate, and so far have not managed to get through to mankind.

Time will tell, and as mankind improves his communications with us, his capability to receive our thoughts will change his life, as the telephone has done. It is a similar comparison, because although at present many cannot hear us, the telephone is a link, an auditory link of communication between two people who cannot see one another, and therefore, although we can see you, the channel, but you cannot see us, it is a similar link in communication, and time will reveal much more to man eventually. I said to you that in time, the power of thought will become so strong that you will be able to improve your surroundings through thought, helping you to overcome any cold in winter by creating a warm surrounding area, and in travel, if there is mist or fog ahead of you, you will be able to overcome this through thought, and create a clear space around you for some way ahead of your vehicle, so that you can travel without danger.

All this is to come, including teleportation, as I have said, so change is all about you, and there is much to look forward to in the future. You and others like you who are able to accept this, will be able to spread the word to one another, and in time to come, more will have open minds and be ready to accept new ideas and concepts about the future, about the changes that will happen on the Earth before very long.

What you need to do now is to spread the word to others about bringing down white light from the Christ Star, and bringing down that vortex of violet flame that is from Saint Germaine and Master R, and the silver that is mixed with it from Grace. It is all linked together, do not worry too much about it, so long as you try to visualise this light filling you, surrounding you and pouring down into the Earth. It helps to raise your consciousness, and to provide a link with the realms above, so that we can come into your aura and create a link, a communication with you, otherwise it is difficult for us to contact you and others of like mind. We will be communicating over the years to come, and creating a corridor of thought between our two worlds, making that link a constant one, so that we can be of help to you in the future, over the time of your transition into the fifth dimension. We only wish to help you in many ways.

My brothers and I are here, linking with you, and are pleased that this first communication has been successful. We hope over the weeks and months to come that we will be able to give you more details to help to bring our wisdom to humanity, and the life you lead here. We give you our blessing, and good wishes for the future, to you and all with whom you work, in service to God. God bless and keep you all. Caristal.

CHANNELLED COMMUNICATIONS FROM PLEIADES CARISTAL-2

I speak to you from that pool of consciousness surrounding the Earth, the Universal Mind. It is Caristal who speaks, and I am happy to greet you again. Our minds are blending together quickly, as you become accustomed to my vibration. We are higher this time, on a higher plane of consciousness, and I am pleased to report that our first communication was a success, and that my brothers were happy with its conclusion.

t is difficult to express myself until I get adjusted to your thoughts. We are all aware that there are few who communicate with Earth dwellers, and it is an exciting time for both you and myself to make this bond between the two planets within the Universe. Our ship is stationary above your home, and like other space beings, I have projected myself into your room in into your aura, your auric space. Both of us are attempting to rise within that vortex of violet flame of light, and the Christ light, working together to channel our minds onto a higher plane. It is a universal thought that those of us from other planets are contacting the Earth at this time, and have been over many years. We project our thoughts into the minds of those who are able to receive them, and from them the instructions or suggestions go forth to others that we can help at this time of change, since we are of a higher evolution than you.

You have been aware of this for some time, that the Earth changes will come to pass, and we are holding ourselves in readiness for this. It is a time when all Earth dwellers will come together in thought and unite, so that you can rise onto a higher plane of consciousness and dimension, together with the Earth. She has been rising gradually, and you and other light workers are attempting to remain with the Earth, rising upwards as she does, so you can find yourselves in a place that is comfortable for you. Not attempting to hold onto the third dimension, but projecting upwards and outwards, keeping your minds open to the full reality of which man is becoming more aware. His and her spiritual nature will develop the ability to become one with the Earth, and with beings from other planets at present unknown to you.

Gradually more beings are becoming able to contact Earthlings. We have been attempting to communicate with others besides you, not always successfully, but we still hope that we can communicate with people right across the world, in time.

It will be a time of rejoicing for mankind, because in his new way of thinking, and in the new dimension, men will be able to communicate with many more beings and civilisations that heretofore have been completely unknown. As I said in my first communication, mankind thought he was the only living being within the Universe. It is only because over the centuries it was thought that humanoids would not be able to survive in other atmospheres, but until the past fifty years there has not been much thought given to the existence of other types of living beings. Some of the children's T.V. programmes have opened the minds of those who watched, to recognise that perhaps other beings could exist in planets, either on the surface as you do, or within the planets as others do, because the outer atmosphere has become impossible to breathe, and that the beings who live upon those planets could be of a completely different structure from your own.

It is only of recent years that more thought has been given to this concept, that perhaps beings could exist in other states other than your own. For instance, as a gaseous nature or liquid, or as I have said before, inside the planets themselves, with buildings, space for living within the structure of the planets, so that the outer air is not necessary.

It is all a new thought for many, although you have been thinking on these lines, and have an open mind, believing in space craft from the very beginning. Many light workers have had the thought that others could live on planets throughout the Universe, and were disappointed when life was not found on Mars and other areas that have been examined by man-made machines, and you realise now that within Mars, Jupiter or Venus there could be beings who are highly evolved species, but constructed differently from you. It is good to have an open mind, and to realise that many beings that are highly evolved, may be completely different or have a similar skeletal structure to your own, but be of a different size, smaller or larger, as the case may be. This has been revealed on T.V. of the Roswell case, where beings had been killed on crash landing many years ago. This was hushed up so that the general public did not know of it, and were misled into thinking it had been a weather balloon. It is strange how people can be misled in this way, because the government wishes them to believe something other than the truth.

There is much that the world governments have covered up in the past that should be brought to light, and if it is not, then we of the Ashtar Command feel that the public of both your country, the United States, Russia, and many others should have television broadcasts made by ourselves, just briefly to put you straight. To give you the truth and state that your governments have been misleading you and that the U.F.O.'s, as you call them, are truly manned by sentient beings who are of good will towards you. There have been some who have abducted humans to do experiments, this was not our intention and never has been, to attempt to understand how humans are constructed, and to use machines to do this. This is not a correct procedure and goes against our principles. But I think that this has all been in the past, and the proceedings have stopped. The 'aliens' were from one particular planet who had no moral principles, unlike ourselves, and who are interested in investigating your planet and Earth dwellers upon it for their own means and purposes. However, all that is in the past, and we will not dwell on these unpleasant topics.

We have many things to discuss with you for the future. Those from our planet wish you well, and we hope in time to come we can keep a link between our planet and your own, so that a constant communication link can be established, and we can receive anything that you wish to broadcast to us. For instance, if help is required, you can let us know in advance what is required, and we can be there within a twinkling of an eye! All these things can come to pass in the future, and your lives will be rewarded by many miraculous happenings. They may seem miraculous to you now, but in the future they will be everyday occurrences, and you will accept these miracles as the norm.

You will be able to transport yourselves in the twinkling of an eye from one country to another, and eventually from one planet to another, in time to come. Everything that will happen is predestined. You will have within you great capabilities, of which you are partly unaware. Your minds are becoming more powerful as you meditate twice daily, and as you use the light over the weeks, months and years, it will become much stronger within you and around you, and you will be able to project this, both for healing and for your own benefit in many ways.

We will go into more details about this in our next communication. For the time being then, I wish you well, and I wish you peace and love from all of us in the Pleiades. God bless, Caristal.

CHANNELLED COMMUNICATIONS FROM PLEIADES CARISTAL-3

I am happy to greet you this day. It is Caristal who speaks, and I know that you are hoping for new revelations on the basic religions of the world. You have read an article that was written by someone in the U.S. air force, someone in authority who had much to say about U.F.O.'s and extra-terrestrial beings. I am very pleased that this article is being passed around, and I hope it will spread the word amongst all who are ready to hear this. It is rather like a thunderbolt, and turns your ideas upside down, something that you have been ready to accept for a while, but until you saw it in print, you had not realised the consequences and the undercurrent within it. I know that you are hoping I will help you in this, and many beings will have their say, their own method of describing the true reality of the past that was written in your Bible and many Holy Books.

Descriptions were difficult in those days for simple men, who described what they had seen, particularly in the Old Testament, things like the burning bush and other descriptions of which you could not understand the full import until you recognised the fact that these various descriptions could have been of space craft landing. In those days it was difficult for anyone to appreciate something so powerful, a sound and sight that was indescribable and unbelievable to them, so they naturally assumed it was God speaking to them, or in fact that it was an Angel or some being of great power. Therefore, all these occurrences were caused by extra terrestrials, including Moses when he went up the mountain and received the Ten Commandments.

I know that all this can be mind boggling, but when you work it out, you can then realise that everything, including Angelic messengers, would be assumed to be other than they were, because mankind could not appreciate there would be other beings alive within the Universe that could visit planet Earth quite easily. They are beings who are highly evolved species compared with mankind, light years ahead of them in thinking and capability, and therefore these simple men wrote down descriptions they could only ally with Angelic Messengers or God, something they could worship from afar. They could not possibly perceive that they were just normal beings from other planets, but in time they accepted everything as gospel, and the truths that were given. Everything was given sincerely, and for instance, the Ten Commandments are upheld to this day, and they are truly good laws that should be used and kept. I know mankind in general is good, and they try to keep the laws, it is only certain elements that ignore these rules, and do what they wish to do rather than the law of the country or government.

Many things in the past have to be reflected upon and weighed up by you now. You have much to consider. All your religions are based on occurrences that like Jesus' life, happened many centuries ago, almost two thousand years now, and everything is based on the Christmas Story of the babe being born in the stable, and the Star above shining down on that stable. He was a Son of God, and truly he was a good and great being, and lived a life that you would do well to use as an example for anyone. He created miracles in his time, and he was truly sincere, everything he said was true, but if you reflect on his birth at that time, if you think of the shining Star that the shepherds watched, and the three wise Kings followed, think of that star as being a shining space craft. Could it not be so? Everything now must be coloured by this thought! Therefore, the being called Jesus could be a new small being born to Mary, but having come from another planet.

You must recognise the fact that many of you have lived on other planets, and have experienced life upon them, and is an entirely different lifestyle from that of the Earth. Try to open your minds further to take in these thoughts, because I and my brothers from the Pleiades are attempting to give you secrets that have been withheld for centuries. Some people have been given knowledge over the past few years that has been given from those like ourselves, who live on other planets of the Universe. You know this and have read certain books channelled by others. We have been working with mankind over the centuries; we have walked amongst you, although perhaps unseen. Our ships have been travelling to and from the Earth, and the surrounding planets for some time, as I said before. We amongst the others who have worked with mankind, are ready now to pass on these truths, you will hear them repeated in different ways from other beings. We only wish you well, and we do not wish to disturb you in any way. That is why we have withheld this knowledge until you are ready to accept it.

There is so much to tell you that we will have to work out the sequence to make it easier for you. You know that the one true God, the Source of all beings is still the God of all. That much is the truth. He is the Creator of all things, and apart from that being of light, your religion has been based on different truths. The truth that you believed in is no longer justified, apart from the fact that Jesus was a great being, a good being who exemplified love. There is no real basis for the Christian religion as such. This is the difficult part because it will throw confusion amongst so many, that it is difficult to know how to put it. Each religion is based on a different being, but each of these beings such as Buddha and Allah, all of them were beings from other planets, and they have been deified. All of them were good men, and all have set a good example to those who worship them and the true God, but religion must be based on truth, and the only truth there is, is that these beings landed on your planet many centuries ago in different parts of your world.

The Earth herself has seen many religions, and it is difficult to destroy these thoughts on which you have based your lives and prayers. Always pray to God as we do, the Creator. We will try to help you periodically, to build up a better and truer basis for your beliefs. Do not feel bereft, but accept the fact that God has many messengers who work for Him, those beings of light the Archangels, who have been working to help mankind over the millennia. They are great beings of peace and love, and Michael the Archangel has been doing much over these centuries to uplift the thought of mankind, as has Sananda and other beings of light. He, who was Jesus in the past, came to Earth to set an example in that life, and his planet of origin was Venus. All these things are true, and we know that you must have something to hold onto, we do not wish you to be bereft of any religion at all. We will try to explain over the next few communications how we and others have been passing on this arcane knowledge to various members of your society.

As time goes by, and you continue to work with the light as we do, you will find that your capabilities will improve in many ways. All you light workers are increasing your ability to rise into a higher dimension, and as you do so, everything will be made clear to you. You will in time be on a similar dimension to us, the fifth dimension, some who are visiting the Earth are on the sixth dimension, but this matters not, because once you have raised onto that higher level, you and the Earth will be part of our plan, and part of the whole cosmic community. Most of us have been working with light for many centuries, and this is how we have evolved a higher vibratory rate and higher capabilities, and once you have reached those, there is no limit to what you can do and how you can travel. We have been travelling interdimensionally, and through time for so many centuries that it is difficult to describe to you the true difference from three-dimensional living to five-dimensional living.

You have much to look forward to, and we will be happy to help you in this new outlook. You and others like you are part of the plan for humanity. Do not look back, always look forward, and you will recognise that you will see things with new eyes, and have completely different thoughts on life and its purpose, and the communications between us can be constant. All is well. We will do all we can to help you and we send you our greetings and love this day. God bless, Caristal.

CHANNELLED COMMUNICATIONS FROM PLEIADES CARISTAL-4

I am here once again to speak to you, this is Caristal, and I give you my best wishes today, and those of my brothers from the Pleiades.

We have much to talk about, and I am pleased that your communication from the U.S.A.F. is being spread around, because it is that truth that we wish to spread throughout the world. The truth that there are many evolved beings communicating with the Earth, who have been either upon the Earth or travelling around it for millennia. We have travelled through space and time to visit your planet, amongst others, and to send forth knowledge and wisdom over the centuries past to those who were able to receive our thoughts, and to communicate in other ways, which perhaps you might not have thought about. It has been known that we have existed over the centuries beyond your knowledge of space, before the time of your knowledge of us, and before your astronomers discovered the many planets, stars and galaxies.

Nevertheless over time, mankind has been developing from when he first came upon the Earth. In the days of Lemuria and before that, humanity began in a different way from at present. As you know, in those days he was closer to God, and he was more like us, able to rise off the planet by various means. It has been hinted in the past that in those days, mankind had the ability to fly, but it was perhaps thought that he had discovered a means of flight by small machines. It has been suggested that perhaps he could fly by teleportation, because in those days when in a more amorphous state, man would be able to use the fourth dimension rather than the third, and find that everything was less dense. Leave it to your imagination, but think of this, because over the centuries and millennia, mankind has changed. In those days life was simple, and he lived with other men without any violence, but there have been changes in the thoughts of man, and those first humans were part of the plan, the Cosmic Plan. Some were created by those beings from other planets. It has been suggested at times that this occurred, but humanity did not wish to believe this.

He believed that he was created in the image of God, which he was, because humanity is perfect in that way, but it is the way that he has evolved through time, with thoughts of violence and causing pollution to the Earth, as time has gone by, that things are getting out of hand in this respect. Humanity must realise that there must be a change of heart, so that the Earth is preserved in the state it is in, and not get any worse. We, and others are here to help at this time, and we have been suggesting that changes be made in the laws, so that by-products from industry no longer pollute the rivers and oceans. This has been noted, and the governments of the world are attempting to change the laws and create a more beautiful Earth as a result. It is essential that these laws are kept, and that there is no further pollution, and that the Earth is cleansed. You who work with the light have been attempting to redress this balance, by bringing light into the Earth, and everything upon it, and this is finally helping to take effect on the pollution that exists. In the past, other planets have had problems of a similar nature, and have had to take drastic action to prevent any further damage.

As I mentioned in my last communication, beings from other planets have visited the Earth over the centuries, and in the days when Jesus walked the Earth, many miraculous happenings occurred, and humanity looked up to these beings of light such as Jesus, and other religious leaders. There have been changes in the thoughts of man since those times, but nevertheless, these religions have continued, and are at the very core of your existence for most of you. I hope that my last communication did not disrupt your views too unkindly, because I would not wish to cause any harm or distress to anyone. I was only trying to point out various facts that had happened in the past. There is a different attitude towards visitations from spacecraft nowadays, and although there have been abductions in the past which caused great alarm, this was only one small section of beings, and they have been stopped from experimenting with any beings from here or any other planets. It is only those who are benign who visit you now, and who wish you well.

It is strange to think that over the centuries, so few have been seen, but we have been working during that time on other dimensions, as you know, and therefore do not have to be seen unless we wish to be. There are many of you who have seen spacecraft periodically, and have not been alarmed by this, because you know that we wish you well, and we only hope that humanity will become accustomed to our presence, knowing it is for your own good that we are here. We help the beings on other planets too, and have been doing so for many centuries past. That is part of our task, and those of many other 'space people' throughout the universe. As you know, we work together in a large team under Ashtar, who is leading many projects concerning the Earth. He is also working with Sananda and other beings of light. The Masters of the Hierarchy sometimes link with us, but we work constantly with Sananda and Michael the Archangel, and occasionally Saint Germaine.

All of us are working with light as you are, and we have been using the violet fire for many, many years. You have just recently begun to use this light, and I think that in time you will find it will help you to rise onto that higher dimension. It takes a little time, but in general you will find that it is quite powerful, and you will gradually project into that fourth dimension without any problems. It is a healing light, and in time you will find the healing process will be much more powerful than before. The white light from the Christ Star has been pouring into the Earth, and is taking effect as more of you find it easier to project this light.

Our communications with the Earth are becoming stronger, and I find that my link with you, the channel, is becoming easier as time progresses. We must both work at this, and try to raise even higher into that superconscious level, which is sometimes difficult to reach and retain, for those on the third dimension, but I am sure that as you work with this light, the violet fire, it will burn away any negative thoughts, and help you in many ways. All of you are doing well, and we from the Pleiades are attempting to communicate with more of you as time goes by. Perhaps several of you who read these words will be able to communicate with us eventually, and we will have many channels in this part of the world. This would be good, because then we can help you even more powerfully, and the more of you who work with us the better.

Sometimes you wonder when the changes will come about on Earth. Those changes that will bring you onto the fifth dimension, and which may be violent. It is something you wonder about and perhaps dread, but you will find that it will be a gradual process. In due course, you and the Earth will have risen to that higher dimension, and you will be able to see us, and all who are working with us, when that time comes. We look forward to this as it is much easier to communicate with someone who can see you as well as hear you, and makes it easier for the person doing the channelling. It is so difficult to visualise a being within your aura who is speaking through your mind. Your thoughts are changed to those of the others' thoughts, and therefore it is a rather nebulous communication compared with actually seeing the being standing there in front of you.

In time your Earth will be a better place to live in. It will be as it was when humanity first came here, the violence will have gone, and all feelings of negativity dissipated completely. The violet fire of light will achieve much of this, but also once you have achieved a higher dimension, positive thoughts and pure light will be your constant companions, because violence cannot live in that rarified atmosphere. It is completely dissipated, and those who have violent thoughts and acts will be thrown aside. They will no longer live upon the Earth in that higher dimension; they cannot exist in these conditions.

So all will be well, there will be peace throughout the land, and you and your loved ones will live in peace and security for the rest of your lives. Think of that, and believe it because it is the truth. There will be a sea change, and over the horizon there is a great new life for all of you. We are helping to bring this about, together with yourselves and others working for the light, both on your world and the realms above. We look forward to our next communication, but in the meantime, we give you our blessings and love to you and all who work with you. Caristal.

CHANNELLED COMMUNICATIONS FROM PLEIADES CARISTAL-5

Yes it is I, Caristal who greets you this day, and wishes you well. We hope that our communications are approved of by you, and those who work with you. I know that there have been controversial subjects brought to bear, but nevertheless it is the truth, and truth will always come to the surface, you cannot hold it back. This is what we deal with, and we hope that as time progresses, we can cover many subjects.

Today I wish to speak to you on several things at this time. We have spoken of spacecraft being shown to the general public periodically, and gradually being accepted as part of life. All this has been occurring over the centuries, and millennia for that matter, because time travel has existed with our civilisation for so long that the years are innumerable, and therefore, over that time we have travelled both into the future and into the past. As a result, as I think I mentioned, we have been seen in Biblical times, which was indescribable to people then, but hopefully not too frightening, because much work has been done in the past, and will be in the future. It is just a question of accepting everything, keeping your mind open to all possibilities.

You have been aware that time travel could exist partly because of, shall we say, conditioning from television programmes and books that have been written on this. The first of which I would think would be H.G. Wells, who wrote of the time machine, and I think this was made into a film, but this has been known of for many years. I hope that you accept this, because time travel has existed and will continue to exist forever. You can visualise time being a moving belt that can move in both directions. This was thought of as the fourth dimension at one time, and I suppose this could be, but it is usually on the fifth dimension that time travel can take place, and teleportation as has been mentioned previously by Sananda and myself. As you know, we work together, Sananda and other beings from planets known and unknown to you. We work with Ashtar Command, for he and others of his kind have been working together for many years. All of us are working for the good of the whole, and to serve God, and to help to pass on our wisdom to those upon Earth and other planets who are at the same stage as Earth and your inhabitants.

When we speak of the Earth, we are aware that perhaps the Earth has not adapted to our dimension yet. We are aware that the Earth herself is gradually rising upwards, but we speak of Earth in general and its inhabitants, yourselves and other beings who live upon the planet. Humanity and the animal kingdom, all that exists upon the Earth is important to us, and we attempt to protect it at all times. We will continue in this way always in the future, so you know that there are many beings, many great beings as well as ourselves who are protecting yourselves and other beings on other planets at the same time. Michael the Archangel has also been mentioned, he is one who has served God for so long, and you are aware that he works with the light as we do. You are learning to use light in a more powerful way, and we hope that this will take effect and will continue to expand as more people join in with you in working with the light, both the Christ Light and the violet fire of light.

We are a part of the plan for protecting the Solar System and other stars way beyond your knowledge. Over the centuries there have been changes, as you know. There have been supernovae, and there have been new planets discovered that were never known about in the past when Galileo and other astronomers first made a plan of the heavens. Your capabilities are becoming stronger in many ways, but still you cannot see many galaxies that stretch into infinity, and universes of which you are completely unaware. In time to come, all will be revealed to you, and as you move onto a higher level of being, you will be able to see so much more. At present you think that in the future you will be able to see us, our spacecraft and the devic kingdom, and perhaps many beings that at present you have only heard of. This is so, but there are many other things that you will be able to see and understand in the future, such as galaxies, universes, and beings of light that at present you are completely unaware of. This is understandable because you exist on the third dimension and they exist on the fifth, sixth and even higher dimensions that you can only dream about, and try to visualise.

Colours and rays of light that you could not see, and which are rather like the ultra violet and infra red rays, which are finer than the rays of the sun, and the light of the moon that you can see, but they are in other dimensions. You can imagine metallic hues that glow in the darkness, and you might try to visualise this, but it is difficult to describe to those on a lower dimension, and we know that there is so much to be revealed to you. Things that you can only dream about, as I say, but it is an exciting time to look forward to for the future, for all of you. Your capabilities will improve in seeing and hearing. As I have said before, you will be able to see us, and it will be easier for those who channel to see us in front of you as we speak to you telepathically. At present we are only thought, we only exist in your imagination, so to speak, because we are unseen on another dimension, but in time we will become real to you, and I know you have faith in us. You know we are here in existence, but it will be easier when you see us and know what we look like, and how we act towards you.

All of us mean well, and perhaps in the past you have heard that beings from the Pleiades have experimented on mankind. In those days changes were made in the structure of man because he was incapable of continuing on the higher level of being at that time, therefore changes were made in his DNA structure. This has gradually altered, and mankind will be able to redevelop his capabilities and the structure of his being. As he develops telepathically and clairvoyantly, and raises his consciousness to the level that he was able to reach when man first lived upon the Earth, then his DNA structure will alter, and return to the way it was in the past. He will be able to do many things in the future, more complex than you have ever known. It is hard for me to describe this in detail, but you know that some people have an awareness that others can only imagine, an awareness of their divinity and be closer to God than most of you.

They are mainly those who are capable of causing miracles to occur. They have an inner knowledge, and they can do many things that others have not yet been able to achieve in their lifetime. These are beings who have been living on other planets in the past, and have reincarnated here. They are evolved, more evolved spiritually than most of you, but in the future you too can have this capability, and gradually man will evolve into a finer being. Time will tell as to how man evolves, and will gradually become more like us. You are true beings of light within, but in time to come, that light will shine forth more powerfully from you, and you will be able to use light to great effect. The auras of those who are highly evolved are extremely bright. They are golden and glowing, and in time to come, your auras will also glow more brightly, and be like theirs, as you too evolve your souls and your spiritual capabilities.

All of us have been working to this end to help you to understand how to reach that higher level of consciousness. I know that you have not been aware of us, but nevertheless, we can be around you and living near you without you necessarily being conscious of our presence. It is difficult to describe to you how this can be, because perhaps you always think you would sense someone in a room or your house, or nearby in the garden, but that is normally on your own dimension. You can be aware and sense things, but when someone is on a higher dimension; then it is not always possible to know there are people or beings around you. We are not trying to enforce our thoughts, but place our thoughts in your minds as I am doing now with this channel who speaks my thoughts, as I think them towards her. I am within her aura, and can project my thoughts in a way that you might not understand, but they can be accepted quite freely, and as time progresses, it has become easier to do so.

I know there are many of you who in the future will be able to receive thoughts from others quite freely, and as you raise your consciousness higher onto the superconscious level, those of you who can receive your guides or the I AM presence or your higher self, will gradually be able to receive our thoughts and those of other beings of light, and in time, channel these thoughts to others. This will be good because it means that our truth will be spread more freely and widely, and as a result, we will be able to help you to raise upwards onto that higher dimension of being, which you are attempting to do at present. This time of change has been gradually creeping up on you. Some of you had it mentioned to you over the last decade, and others for even longer. Time has elapsed quite quickly it seems to you, but now time is running short, and this is the time that we have been talking about, that of when the Earth changes happen.

    This can be quite a gradual process if you will accept this change, and continue to try to raise yourselves higher as the Earth does. All of you light workers have been aware of this transition phase for some time, and I know that you maybe feel daunted by the prospect when you realise that the time is now or soon enough. Be brave and bold, and go about this in a confident manner, knowing that you are being protected by beings of light, and no harm will come to you, or those whom you love. It is a time of great change, and great joy for you and all who work with you. Be thrilled at the thought of this change, and know that all who are working with the light are with you in this. I, Caristal, and my brothers from the Pleiades wish you well, and we look forward to our next communication. God bless and keep you all.

CHANNELLED COMMUNICATIONS FROM PLEIADES CARISTAL-6

This is Caristal, and I wish to greet you all this day with my love and good wishes. I hope that as time progresses, we will feel closer in thought and action. My thoughts are sent forth through another, as you know, and sometimes it is difficult to establish that rapport, and be able to say exactly what I wish to, in a short space of time. Gradually we are becoming one in thought, and this way of speaking to you all is becoming the norm for many beings from other planets. We are relaying our thoughts through others, and establishing a foundation of truth for earth dwellers. All of us wish you well, and we have been establishing many centres throughout the Earth. The spacecraft that we use do not land on the Earth; when communicating, we project ourselves down into the house of those who channel our thoughts. We come into the aura of that person, and are therefore able to use their minds for our purposes, the channel does not go into a trance, but just allows our thoughts to drop into her mind. Some who channel may do so, but not this particular one.

We have much to tell you over the ensuing months, news of many beings who have been circling the Earth, ready for changes that will occur in the Earth's structure and in humanity. You know that we have been visiting the Earth for so long, that it is unnecessary for me to establish this fact with you. The Pleiadeans have done much work with Earth dwellers, and will continue to be closer to you over the years. We and those from Arcturus and Sirius, and many other planets known and unknown to you, are all working together as you know. There is talk from other channels, saying there will be mass landings from spacecraft, and that the craft will land on your planet, and there will be many space beings landing here on Earth.

We do not go along with this, and it is perhaps what certain people have channelled. We have been around, as I have said before, for many hundreds of years, and we have not been seen, we work on another dimension. As mentioned, we have been around you on your planet, talking through peoples' minds, and trying to establish a rapport between us, but you, and others like you until now have mostly been completely unaware of us. We do not necessarily have to have mass landings of space vehicles in order to help those on your planet, as might have been suggested, and we do not have to be here in such numbers that humanity will be overrun or frightened, that is not our purpose. We are only here to help and advise you, and we do not wish to have craft landing all over the Earth, that is not our way, or the ways of those with whom we work. We have been circling the Earth for so long. Some of us have shown our vehicles now and again, but it is not necessary for all of us to land in large numbers.

When the changes come, you will be rising upwards onto the higher dimension, and therefore if there are any dangers on the Earth, you will have raised upwards onto that higher dimension, and you will be protected, as a result. You and your families will be safe, and you will be given plenty of warning if there is any danger in your area. What is necessary is for mankind to raise his consciousness daily, and try to think of himself as rising on a beam of light upwards, so that his consciousness is aware it is raised from the mundane level of existence, meeting us half way, or fully, so that you are ready to move into that higher dimension on the higher vibration. This is the most important factor at this time, and I feel that this is to be impinged on your minds. Do not think of us landing and taking you away to safely to another planet or something similar, this is not our way. All that we need is for you to do your part, and that change will come to you quite easily, but it is from you, not changes that will come about through our landing and removing you from the planet.

So, once you have risen onto the fifth dimension, in time, your bodies will have changed, so that you can remove yourselves from any third-dimensional danger. I feel sure that when that time comes, you will have discovered your new capabilities when you are on the fourth dimension, and once this is achieved, the necessary change onto the fifth will be much simpler. You will be capable of so many more things than you are at present, and your clairvoyance as we might call it will be outstanding, because your inner eye will be opened fully, and be aware of beings who are all around you when you walk through the countryside, and in your gardens. At present they are hidden from you on that higher dimension. As time progresses, they will be seen clearly by you, and you will be thrilled at the sights you will be able to see. That invisible world will be opened to you, that veil will be lifted, and all these beings who are ethereal to you at present will become completely visible.

Some people are able to fleetingly see glimpses of these beings if they are clairvoyant, but once you have achieved this higher dimension, a whole new world will be open to you, and what children can often see, and that you may have seen as a child, will be revealed to you in all its splendour. The colours of these beings are magnificent, and have sometimes been described to you. The devas are fountains of light and colour, and all the angelic stream of consciousness will be seen periodically as you rise onto higher dimensions, but that is for the future. Now is the time when you have to prepare for this new vision, and to be ready to accept it, and to tell others. Try to plant a seed of knowledge in their minds that there is another world that they are a part of as spiritual beings, and which if they wish to learn about, they can if they will just be still and close their thoughts, and allow other thoughts to be dropped into their minds in meditation. It is a difficult thing, to broach this subject with others, who perhaps have not thought in this way before, but I think that gradually over time to come, if all of you spiritually minded people will pass on this fact gradually, humanity will be ready to move upwards with the Earth as she changes, and comes onto the fifth dimension with the other planets, who have been evolving over past millennia.

My brothers and I wish to help you, and we only hope all of you will feel that we are of like mind. There are stories of beings, who have come in spacecraft and abducted humans in the past, but this is all in the past, and those operations and investigations are finished. They were beings who have come from other planets, but these are not allowed to visit Earth now. Experimentation has been banned and all of us are working for the good of mankind, to help him to change his ways, and to raise his thoughts and minds to that new level of consciousness. We wish to work for the good of the whole, and we link with Sananda, as you know, and other great beings of light.

Our spacecraft have rarely been seen by Earth dwellers, but at times there have been sightings, both of our craft and those from other planets. They vary in size and shape, and they vary in the fact that they can be cloaked whenever we wish, so that sometimes you may see a craft in the distance, and wonder whether it is truly a spacecraft. As a rule, it will be, and over the years to come, you may see more, because I think that mankind now understands that we are only here to help, and that there is no danger. It will be like seeing a plane in the sky, or a car on the road, and will become quite mundane over the years to come, but nevertheless, we will not be having mass landings. Only if it is really essential, will some people be saved from any disaster, and we may have to swoop down to help, but generally speaking, you will be changed physically when the Earth changes occur, and gradually you will be raised onto that higher level and be like ourselves.

We have been on a higher dimension ever since we have been aware of our existence, and therefore it has not been any effort for us to travel through space and time to visit your planet, but in due course you too will have this capability, and your lives will become freer as a result. It is something to look forward to and your lives will be utterly changed in so many ways. There will be more time for leisure, and less work from nine to five. Alterations will happen gradually, and in time, people will come to accept this new thought of a different lifestyle for all. Your world will become a place of peace and stability, and beauty will be all around you. Never fear, protection will be given to you during this time of transition, and you will be blessed by the knowledge that God is working through us all, and guiding our ways to the ways of peace. All is well; we will protect and guide you. God bless and keep you all, Caristal.

CHANNELLED COMMUNICATIONS FROM PLEIADES CARISTAL-7

I Caristal speak to you this day, and I realise that the time has come for mankind to change his ways. There comes a time when man must change, and this is the time you have been waiting for, when man must tidy his affairs, and re-arrange his thoughts in different ways from those in the past. Those who are adjusted to this new way of understanding are gradually raising their consciousness and expanding it at this time, but there are many who are not ready, and must be prepared for change in so many ways in their lives. Children are now being born who are ready for this, but they have to grow and become adult before they can begin to teach those whom they have come to help. There are some people who are now leading the way, and are the vanguard for those who follow, teaching all with whom they come in contact, unafraid of seeming different because this is something that can hold you back. Very few are ready to stand up and be counted, as they say, very few are ready to be a different breed or type, or to stand out in a crowd and be prepared to say what it is that is necessary at this time.

We Pleiadeans have been channelling our thoughts for some time, as you know, through more and more individuals who are ready to receive and voice our thoughts. They have been working in faith, and all of you who are aware of your capabilities must also work in faith, and help to prepare those who are unaware of their potential, by explaining how to raise their consciousness in order to be ready for this ascension to a higher dimension. This time of change is causing a stirring amidst you, and increasing numbers of you are aware of presences, both of ourselves from other planets, and of the presence of the devic kingdom, guides, or more able to hear that still small voice from within. It all takes time, and although so many of you have been meditating once or twice daily over the years, it needs dedication and faith that all this is coming to pass, so that humanity and the Earth are about to take a giant step into the fourth and then the fifth dimension.

It is quite daunting I know, and we can perceive your hesitation, and that although you wish to take this step, it is a step into the unknown that can be difficult to take, particularly when it has not been achieved before, apart from those who are Avatars. We know what it is to be on the fifth and sixth dimensions, but we appreciate and have great sympathy for you at this time. This is why more of us are attempting to help, to give power to you, and give you our support. We and those with whom we have been working, such as Sananda, other Masters of the Hierarchy and the Angelic Hierarchy, and our Leader from 'space' as you call it, Ashtar, all are attempting to help you to achieve what you wish to achieve, that step that is waiting to be taken. Some of you recently have felt very close to achieving this dimension, you have risen upwards on a beam of light; you have walked up lighted stairways, and have tried to go through the doorway of light that leads you to that higher dimension.

You are extremely near, and you are ready to achieve this mastery, it just takes a little time, and I know that although you feel ready to do so, there is a moment of choice, and sometimes you retract your spiritual self away from that doorway of light. You feel you have entered, but not quite, it will happen, believe me, and soon without any effort at all. It will happen in a blinking of any eye, and you will not have realised until you can see many things that at present are invisible to you, like ourselves on another dimension, and sometimes from another time, but that can complicate things when you try to think of too much at once. Just think of it as another dimension, and realise that potential that you have is there waiting to be utilised, and you will see many glorious sights once you have taken that bold step forward.

Things that we have known about, seen, and taken for granted will have the veil lifted away from you, where they have been hidden from view. Many things that we cannot conceive, that you cannot see, but we realise that you cannot. They are too numerous to mention by name, but in time you will realise what you have been missing all your lives. Beings have existed alongside you, who are completely invisible to you, both large and small. In fact, some are minute, but beautiful; I will wait for you to see them yourselves, because the secret would be half revealed if I described them to you in detail.

There are many large bulky objects that you have been unable to see, except very occasionally, and then only by certain people, these are spaceships large and small, and of different shapes. This is something that you might not have thought of, but you will be able to see them constantly once your reach that higher dimension, because many are cloaked from view presently, and this is deliberate, since we do not wish to alarm humanity more than necessary at this time, although spacecraft have been visiting the Earth and many other planets over the millennia. As mentioned, they have been described in the Bible in rather a strange manner, but something from the future, from another planet would be inconceivable to those two or three thousand years ago, unless they were aware that very advanced beings had lived temporarily on the planet Earth, and had bases there, where they had built many structures.

These craft have been transporting us through space and time over these thousands of years, quite invisible most of the time, but once you have achieved that higher dimension, most of them will be visible to you, and this will be another sight that will be quite exciting for you, apart from all the other beautiful beings. Our craft are rather beautiful in their own way, and you will be able to see them quite closely, whereas sometimes when you have glimpsed them, they have been at a distance, and moved away very swiftly into another dimension, usually quite silently. Now the time has come for mankind to be able to accept all these new things, all these changes that will come about soon. You and others who read these words should try to put in a word here and there about your new way of thinking, and how most people will have to adjust to the new conditions that will arise.

Lives will be changed, not unduly for you, but they will be changed for the better for all. Life will become more peaceful and leisurely for everyone, including those who are presently working, both in industry and in everything that is concerned with making money. That will no longer be necessary. Perhaps this sounds a very bald statement, or bold statement shall we say, but nevertheless it will in time be completely true. There will be no necessity for anyone to go out to work. There will be such a change in attitude, that you will be able to perform miracles as it would seem to you now, but through the mind, you will achieve so much that at present is done manually. There will be achievements that you could not conceive of at present. The mind is capable of so much more than you can ever imagine.

At present you are using your minds to bring down light, and to send light to places where there is violence. You are sending healing light to those who need help, but also in the future you will use your minds to create many things, the mind is only partially used at present. It is rather like an iceberg, where nine tenths of it are hidden below the surface, and so the mind that is presently being used is only one tenth of what can be the potential for creating so many useful products. I will leave it at that, because time will tell, and you will discover your endless capabilities when you learn how to use your mind to the full, for the good of yourselves and everyone with whom you come in contact. We use our minds to create small vehicles, to create certain foodstuffs and liquids, and all manner of things. I leave it to your imagination, but you will realise that money will be superfluous.

It would be like being in a world where there was devastation everywhere. I am not saying that this will happen to the Earth, but visualise a situation where you have saved thousands of pounds, shall we say. The money is in a bank or building society. If all these places were razed to the ground and there was nothing, no shops, nothing that money could buy, what use will your money be then? I do not mean that this will happen to the Earth, I am just giving you an example where money would be utterly useless to anyone under these circumstances. If the mind is used to its full potential, when you are on that higher dimension, you will realise that the mind is all that is necessary, and you can provide whatever you need.

Think on these things, and try to assimilate these new thoughts for the future. You and other spiritually awakened people who will be reading these words, and with whom you work, will appreciate how things will change radically in future days. I am not saying that this will happen, all of it within a month or two, but it will occur soon within your

time. I am sure that you will look forward to the changes to come once you become accustomed to these new thoughts, and appreciate how conditions will improve as you learn your new capabilities. All who are in the ethereal realms will give you help, and once you have expanded your consciousness fully to join with us, we will be able to help you all the more. In the meantime, God's blessing be with you all this day, and always.
Caristal.

CHANNELLED COMMUNICATIONS FROM PLEIADES CARISTAL-8

I Caristal greet you all this day, all workers for the light who read these words. Over the last year many of you have been experiencing changes, perhaps unnoticed for a while, but you may find that you have felt pain periodically, pain either in the head or limbs, maybe fleeting, but these are changes that are coming to pass to those of you who are attempting to raise your consciousness, particularly at this time. You are preparing yourselves for the changes that are coming throughout the Earth, and these changes are physical, both in the Earth and you, not undue change, but change nevertheless, and as a result your bodies are preparing for this in subtle ways.

You have heard perhaps that in the past your DNA was altered by us, by those who came from the Pleiades, and that changes were wrought upon your being. It is perhaps true that this did occur, but now there is a change within you. Your DNA is changing and growing, because through channelling our thoughts and those of other beings of light, a change is being made in your DNA, and you are being made capable of more rapport between ourselves and yourselves, and through this there is growth, both spiritual and physical. It may be difficult to accept but it can be proved in future years if tests are made, and there will be results from this to prove that the DNA has altered over recent times. You may not ever have these tests, but accept the fact that through reaching your consciousness to a higher level, and being in contact with beings of light, your DNA has grown to a higher percentage than before. As a result of this, you will be capable of more contact between yourself and other beings of light, and the more that you are in communication with them, the more you will find that your capabilities improve.

There are many people now who are in contact with us and other members of the Pleiades, and those other planets who are presently helping Earth dwellers, all who have been in communication with us will find their consciousness has expanded, so that in time to come, that coming change in dimension will be easier for you. You will be ready to accept this, ready for that step into the unknown that you feel rather hesitant about taking. We are aware of this, and we are attempting to help all of you at this time, and those who are channelling our thoughts to others are being prepared for this. They may not realise this at present, but their consciousness has expanded and will continue to do so, until that time when you are able to access the fourth dimension, and then quite swiftly following that, the fifth dimension where we dwell, and also partly on the sixth dimension.

Others from the Pleiades have been joining me and experiencing what I have experienced, that of watching you and others like you living your lives on this three dimensional Earth, and attempting to reach up onto the spiritual realms through your meditations. Those of us who are from the Pleiades have not had to do this during our lives, because our capabilities have been there with us constantly. We use thought to communicate always, and therefore it is of great interest to us to watch you when you meditate, and are extremely impressed in the dedication you have to do this work. More of you who read these words are meditating twice daily now, and attempting to raise your consciousness more frequently, and this is good, because it means that you will find that linking with the mind will become second nature to you soon. Once you have raised onto that higher level you will find that thought will become all powerful, and that through thought you will transfer your thoughts to others, both on the third dimensional world in which you live, and to those of us with whom you will link more readily when the time comes, and you are on that higher dimension of being.

We have noticed that your capabilities are improving, although you may not have realised this yourselves. Of recent times, you have been able to rise upwards quite quickly now, on that beam of light, to reach us more readily. By us, I do not necessarily mean myself and other Pleiadeans, but any being, your guide, higher self or indeed Master or Angelic Beings. It matters not whoever you are attempting to communicate with or link with. You are finding it easier to link your mind with theirs.

Over the centuries that we have been visiting the Earth we have found that changes have been gradually taking place within the earth dwellers. I of course have not been visiting the Earth very long, but I have heard from others that in the past, very few contacts have been made with Earth dwellers, whereas over the last two decades there has been much more communication between ourselves and yourselves.

Time is getting short, and it is imperative that we communicate with more and more who will accept our thoughts and guidance. We have great experience, and have had experience with other planets in the past, in helping at transition times, and this is a time of transition for your planet, and those upon it. I think you have been told this before by other beings, so I will not dwell on the fact, but we only wish to help you and guide others who you will tell. You have all this wealth of knowledge within you; all of you, and you only have to turn within to find it. This is something that many of you are discovering, and perhaps have known about for some years, but if you turn within, you will be capable of knowing so much more. You can read books about many esoteric subjects that are being printed nowadays. Those books are perhaps coming from people who have learnt to turn within and gain that knowledge, that wisdom of the ages, the ancient wisdom that is known to us, and to all who have worked with us. You can learn this if you will listen to that inner voice speaking to you. It is sometimes from the Universal Mind, sometimes from your guide, or another being who is trying to help you, so long as you protect yourself with light and an invocation is said, all is well and you can turn within and hear our thoughts.

All of you are being guided at this time, and we from the Pleiades are happy to be a part of God's Plan, and to help you and many others. I, Caristal, know that your minds have great potential, and that you have discovered that through thought you can send forth healing. I mentioned this in my last communication I think, and that thought will become the most important factor in the future. It is important that your thoughts are used for good always, never project thoughts that are evil or not of good intent. It is important to watch this always, because as I said before, it can be a great force that should always be used for the good of all, and in time to come, the power of thought will create many useful things. I know that you cannot conceive how this will be in detail, because at present your thoughts have been used solely to bring down light and healing. You have used thought for the good in this work, but believe me, the power of thought can be utilised for many things.

Power is used by the mind by us to create everything we need. Our planet is different from yours, of course, and although we are not living on it presently, we have many things that have been produced by us on our spacecraft, that could not otherwise have been brought from the planet. Thoughts can provide many needs, and in the future this will be an important part of your lives, so that industry will not be required when those changes come. Everything will be altered to a new way of living, and you will find yourselves with much leisure time on your hands, but it can be used to good advantage, both for yourselves and others, and you will be able to speed through thought across great distances, teleportation will become an everyday occurrence. The days of waiting in queues for public transport will be over, and so many people will find great happiness in this, I am sure! You have only to use your imagination to realise how things will change, so you will not have to stand out in bad weather, waiting for a bus! This will be a wonderful change for many millions of people throughout the globe.

However, that is by the way, we know that everything that is changing is for the better for all of you, and for that only time will tell. We trust that you believe in our words, because we would not tell you these things if they were not true. The end of darkness and violence will come, and you will see the dawning of a true new age for mankind. What you have known in the past will dwell in the past, and wars will end for good and all. I know you cannot imagine how this will come about, but it will, and the future looks bright for all of you. You and your loved ones have so much to look forward to at this change, this transition time in the Earth's history. Have faith in us, and you will find that it will be justified, and you can pass on this knowledge to anyone who is ready to receive it. It is the truth, and all will be well. We will watch over you and help you in any way. God bless, Caristal.

CHANNELLED COMMUNICATIONS FROM PLEIADES CARISTAL-9

I give you my blessings this day, this is Caristal. I find that gradually our minds are blending together very quickly, and I think that all of you who read my words are learning that their capabilities of linking with other dimensions of being are improving, and gradually your subconscious and superconscious is rising to a higher level. As a result it takes less time to hear that inner voice of whoever is contacting you, your higher self, guide, other being, or God, the I AM presence. Anything is possible, and particularly now, when the time of transition is upon the Earth and those who dwell upon it.

This time of change is something for which you have waited for some time, and those who have been spiritually aware for two decades may have thought the time would never come, because promises were made by beings of light and space beings, that changes would come, and you were beginning to lose faith in us and other beings from other planets, but time is an elusive thing, it is as you know man made, and we exist out of time, therefore it is difficult to prophecy when something will occur in your time. Perhaps those who were spiritually aware so long ago accepted this fact and realised it would happen one day.

Something that has been prophesied always happens, but not always when you expect it, it eventually occurs, perhaps years later, but it does happen, so always have faith in our words, because no one would attempt to pass on knowledge that was untrue. It is only that the time was unripe for mankind or the Earth to change, but many changes have occurred and continuing to do so over the years. The period of time that it has occurred may seem a long time for you, but it is nothing to us, because we, existing on another dimension, travel through time always, and have done all our lives. Therefore, earthly time means nothing to us, so it is rather difficult for us to weigh up whether you have had to wait for many years, or perhaps just a few months for something to occur.

You who read these words are now aware that things are speeding up, and that your capabilities will improve tremendously. Young people have noticed this too, not just older people, and once this has been recognised, people will start noticing many things that have occurred previously, without them being attributed to time. Most who are spiritually aware have open minds, and are curious about strange happenings that occurred over the centuries.

In the past, men have talked about ghostly figures in old buildings, and attributed it to haunting by spirits that have passed on and are perhaps troubled. Maybe they were killed in a tragedy, and they passed into spirit. Sometimes a figure has been seen and disappeared through a wall, and this maybe was frightening for those who have seen it happen. It may have been a spirit, or maybe someone on another dimension who has come through to that house where those people were living, by accident. They may have been time travellers like us, and all of it happened long ago, but showed itself in the present for those who were viewing it. Most of these ghostly apparitions can be explained away if you try to think with an open mind, and someone from the past travelling into the future appeared momentarily in 1995 for instance, and was seen. Or it may be someone who exists in another dimension, perhaps the fourth or fifth, and they could have been from another planet.

I am just trying to expand your mind slightly, like the television programme that some of you watch, where beings from other worlds visit spaceships, and the spaceship crew descend on another planet. All of these things can be the truth, and beings from other planets are naturally different from you, and may not even be similar to the ones on the programme. They could exist without form, without human form, or forms you might expect. They may be just a giant brain, a formless substance like jelly or liquid, or some type of air or gas. Anything is possible on other planets that perhaps you have never heard of. It only goes to show that you should not have preconceived ideas about anything, even ghosts as you might call them, because, although a house may be said to be haunted by ghosts, perhaps time travellers have visited it, and used as a base for them from other planets or dimensions.

So many things are perfectly feasible when you attempt to reason them out with an expanded mind. I know you have heard of lateral thinking, and perhaps this comes into it, but it is good to have an open mind on many subjects, so that you can learn constantly the whole of your lives. It is part of your reward for living. Living a life, incarnating upon any world is part of God's Plan, that is what He wishes all of us to do, in order to continue learning and evolving, both our minds and souls, so that we can be better beings as a result.

This life for you is a very important one, because you are living at this time of change. You have chosen to come upon the Earth to learn through this incarnation, and you will have experienced very much more by the end of this incarnation, I am sure, than any previous ones. You may have been very experienced in different faculties in the past, perhaps you might have been in medicine, priests, or priestesses in past lives, and been very expert in whatever you did, but this lifetime is different. It is because of the change that is happening for the Earth and all of you who live on it. You are attempting to accomplish something that has not been done before, apart from those who are highly evolved, such as avatars like Sai Baba or Mother Meera, and other beings like them, but you taking part in this new dimension, and you are part of God's Plan.

You have much work to do and are attempting an entirely new experience by reaching to your superconscious level. Your minds are expanding quite rapidly now, and will reach that necessary level of the fourth dimension. It is something you look forward to and will be able to see so many things, and be able to take part in helping others in many ways, both beings of light and those who still exist purely on the third dimension. You will also be on the third, but able to rise to the fourth dimension when you wish. It all takes time and practice, and it will only happen when you are ready for this, so fear not, but have faith and know that you will be capable of this when the right time comes for you.

I have said before, and I repeat this, that thought is all powerful, and that your thought will take you anywhere you wish in time, but that will be when you have reached that higher level of being, once you have passed to the fifth dimension, and you will be capable of much more. Once achieved, it will be simple for you to slip through onto the fifth level, because they are very close together, and once you have entered through that threshold of light onto the fourth, it will be simplicity itself to slip up into the fifth dimension, and be able to use your mind for travel and so many more things of which at present you cannot conceive.

I Caristal, and my brothers from the Pleiades watch over you constantly, and we wish you well. We take a great interest in you all who read the words that we speak through this channel. We know you are earnest in your desire to improve your capabilities, and we truly wish you well. God bless and keep you until we speak again, Caristal.

CHANNELLED COMMUNICATIONS FROM PLEIADES CARISTAL-10

It is good to greet you once more. This is Caristal, and I wish to speak on many subjects over the next few communications. This time of change within the Earth and within mankind is good, because more people are opening their minds to new possibilities. This year will bring more change with it, and we hope that for you it will be for good. It is time that mankind realised his capabilities, and some are beginning to wake up to new ideas. There have been more programmes on your televisions about so-called science fiction, some of it is fiction, and some of it fact. In some small way we hope we too are helping to expand your minds.

It is difficult to broach these subjects to begin with, but more people, particularly in this part of the country, are accepting facts about U.F.O.'s and that there are other sentient beings who must exist within your universe. They are accepting the fact that mankind is not the only being in the universe, and it is possible for different types of beings exist other than humanoid. Much has been accepted that may not have been accepted as truth in the past, U.F.O.'s, that life doesn't end when you 'die', but life continues forever, and life after life as reincarnation.

This is comparatively new for those in the west. As you are aware, the eastern religions have always believed in reincarnation as a fact of life, that the wheel of karma turns constantly, and that each lifetime is a time for the soul to learn new experiences, and evolve further up the ladder of evolution, and each lifetime builds new capabilities into that soul, which has existed over many lifetimes. This is the truth, but it is only of recent years that more western people have recognised and accepted it. Even so, there are thousands who will never believe this, they have closed minds and will not accept new thoughts that do not agree with their past thinking. They will never change in this lifetime, and therefore it is a waste of time talking to them on these subjects, and spirituality is a subject that cannot be conceived of by those with closed minds. They are not at all ready to accept new ideas on religion, and their past beliefs are good enough for them. So, accept this and go along with it, and realise unfortunately this core of people will not continue into the fourth dimension when those on the spiritual path raise onto that new level of being.

Just keep continuing to practice reaching to that portal of light into the fourth dimension, and once passed through you will experience many wonders you are eagerly anticipating, and that is most of you. You may be concerned that you will not keep in touch with loved ones, but trust that all will be well. Be bold and know you can return to the third dimension whenever you wish, until the Earth has moved upto the fourth as well. Just keep raising your consciousness up the shaft of light and you will manage it well.

God is with you in this Plan of His, and He has sent us and His messengers of light, the Angelic Hierarchy, to hep you to reach this new level of being. His plan is for all of you on the spiritual path, and it is part of our task to help you and others of like mind to rise up eventually onto our level of being. Time will tell, and you will find that as the months go by, you will manage to achieve this in due course. All you need to do is have trust, and then know from your heart that everything will take place in due course. Just think on these things and use thought as your guide. As you think about it, so it will be, and you will overcome the fear or doubt through bringing light into yourselves from the Christ Star, and that violet fire of light from St Germaine, that you are using to good effect.

Over the years we have been using light to good effect ourselves. It has accomplished much in our lifetimes. The light we use is what you are using, and also light that has been given to us while we were living our lives on the Pleiades. We and our brothers who are still there have used light for nourishment and healing in many ways. As you know, it is a life force, and can be breathed in and used very powerfully for your own benefit. We have used it as a form of nourishment in the past, and at times we still do so for our own benefit. We have said to you in the past that we could not bring material objects with us on our ships, not as much as you might imagine, because we need to keep these to the minimum, but when we need nourishment of some kind, we use our minds to bring this about through thought, and we can create many things through this process.

Eventually you too will be able to use your thoughts to good advantage to create objects you need, perhaps nourishment, or something to be done for you, such as using thought to cleanse a room, or many things that save you time, so you can use it to better advantage. The time that may be precious to you, although man made, is part of your life on the third dimension, but once you have reached the fourth and fifth dimensions, this thought construction, creativity, whatever you wish to call it, can be used very effectively, so that your lives can be organised in a better way. You can adapt what you do in each day to better advantage for the benefit of others, perhaps in healing, or sending light and love to them in a powerful way. You may need more time to do this than you have to hand, and therefore you can move upto that higher dimension of being where time will be non-existent for you. Your lives will be totally transformed when this happens, and although presently you cannot imagine how it will be, it may not be long before it occurs.

As I said in my last communication with you, this lifetime will prove to be most important. When such a large step for humanity is about to be taken, when you raise onto that higher dimension, and has not occurred since the world began. Therefore, this new experience will create for you a large portion of evolution for your souls. You will find you do not need to return to that wheel of karma, and this will be the last incarnation where you need to repay any karma. Through taking this new step upwards, you will have achieved more than usual in this lifetime, so rejoice to know this and recognise the fact that what you achieve at this time will make a great difference to your evolutionary progress. Your guides and teachers will be learning much at this time also, and moving upwards in their scale of reference. They will learn through you, as you know, and move on to others who are not as far along the spiritual path as you later on.

You may have found this in the past, and now have guides who are more experienced than your previous ones. Some of you have found this, I know, wherever you are at this time is right for you, and you are learning in your own way whatever you need to learn, in whatever manner. In time you will level off, and recognise that this lifetime is one that will demonstrate what can be achieved in one life.

Great things are happening at present, and you are fortunate indeed to be experiencing this. You chose to come to live at this time upon the Earth, and to experience all the changes that have been occurring, and will continue over time. There is much bad press for those transgressors, for the violence and chaos must occur before the good times will come. The Golden Age that will come, and the Phoenix will rise from the ashes eventually, and the Earth will be cleansed of the prevailing negativity.

The real gold in your hearts will be revealed, and all of you who are of like mind, will continue in the true way of life, that of caring and sending out love and healing to others. Those who have a negative outlook and closed minds will not continue, as the Earth moves upwards to the fourth dimension. All will come to pass in time, and you and others like you will be safe. Your loved ones will be protected, and you and your loved ones will find a new beginning, this I promise you, and this New Age will truly begin, the age of new discoveries and capabilities that will change everything, and sweep aside the disasters that have occurred. I will speak again on many things, but in the meantime, my blessing be upon you all, Caristal.

CHANNELLED COMMUNICATIONS FROM PLEIADES CARISTAL-11

I Caristal, wish to speak to you on many things, and are waiting to be voiced. I know you are interested in what I have to say. Your consciousness is gradually rising higher, as all of you these past months. There is a great speeding up in this process through the use of light, and is becoming more powerful, affecting you and your surroundings. The light is necessary to build up that level of consciousness to reach the universal mind, and meet with us on that higher level. As you gradually grow into this new concept, you will recognise the fact that those on Earth are relearning new capabilities that were there many centuries ago. In the past, humanity was capable of much more than at present, and you are relearning that capability that was taken from you in the past. There is a cosmic power building up within the Earth through your working with the light, and I hope soon that you will be able to conceive of what I wish to tell you.

Those of us from other planets and stars who have been visiting the Earth and other planets over thousands of years have been aware Earth has not received its fair share of light, but now you are learning to work with light, you will recognise that in the past, many beings of light have landed on Earth and used Earth as a base. Those of you who are able to recognise this will realise although the Bible speaks of these visitations in biblical terms, the beings who visited Earth in those days were looked upto as God or gods. They were not, however, but highly evolved beings from other worlds who had visited Earth, and used humanity in different ways. Sometimes it was mixing with humanity and teaching them the ways of their worlds, or merging with the female of your species to bring about a new form of humanity who were capable of conceiving more through their minds than the general populace. A new species of humanity was created, and were capable of very much more than in former years.

Much has been spoken on this subject. Also I know you recognise the many buildings etc still extant on the Earth that were created by super humans, and are some of the wonders of the world. Edifices like the Pyramids, Stonehenge and Easter Island, which would have taken many years to build but usual means. They were made by beings from other planets or those humans who were able to raise the structures through sound and other methods.

You know from legends and myths of winged beings and angels of light, who have been spoken of with great awe. Some of these beings have truly been angelic, but others have been beings who have passed the time barrier, or crossed through space in craft as depicted on cave walls by humanity in those days. Some of the extra terrestrials have been from the Pleiades or Sirius, or planets and galaxies unknown to you. Over the millennia the Earth has been visited and used by beings or energies of light, and as a result of this, humanity has changed, and it has known capabilities in the past that are beginning to be realised. As you grow and expand consciousness into the higher capabilities you have within, and must be encouraged, you will recognise humanity had these gifts in the past, and were taken from you. Now you will grow into the beings you truly are, and will be able to join with us to make the Earth what it will be in the future, part of the cosmic creation, playing a full part in joining with us to form a unity of planets working for the light.

We have been trying to help mankind for so long, and it has been a battle with the powers of darkness, but as you will recognise now, we are winning. There is still negativity around that may try to hinder, but the light will prevail, and the darkness has had its day. Try to learn each day how you can expand your awareness, and try to teach others who will accept it, and also link with others who can help you. It has taken so long to bring you out of that long sleep that has been a sad experience for us.

Humanity has been deprived of this light for long enough, and you are able to do many things, and help bring the Earth into that new vibration, and then Earth can become part of the cosmic community.

We link with the Masters of the Hierarchy and Sananda, who has worked for so long for the good of all creation. He, like other great beings of light, came from Venus, and he links with many beings of light at this time, as you are aware, and over the centuries we have helped him, and those who work with him to create a great unity for good throughout this universe and beyond. There are galaxies you cannot conceive of because this 'space' is ever expanding, and there are universes beyond this one that you could not imagine. It goes into infinity, and human minds cannot conceive this, but this doesn't matter as long as you realise we work for good, and we hope in future days, as your capabilities continue to expand, you will join us in this work.

It is necessary for you to realise that you are beings of light trapped in physical bodies in your physical existence, but your consciousness can know no bounds, and it is capable of reaching towards us, and to others who are attempting to help you to waken from the bonds you have been held within over the centuries, so that the light will prevail, and bring about a new awareness that all of you will have, and you will be aware of us and all with whom we work for the good of creation. God bless and keep you all, Caristal.

CHANNELLED COMMUNICATIONS FROM PLEIADES CARISTAL-12

I Caristal am happy to greet you once more. It seems that humanity is at last surging forwards with new ideas, and new knowledge of his capabilities. Many books have been written about spiritual matters, and things that have not been imagined in the past, because people had been fighting a losing battle in attempting to talk about UFO's and other allied subjects to an unbelieving audience, but now there is more acceptance. On TV there is more acceptance, and programmes that were taboo before, are shown, such as hypnosis and supernatural programmes, and also the 'X' files is something many people watch. It may not be to everyone's taste, but it is exploring new topics that have been unaccepted previously. Therefore, we have also been accepted more in the minds of men, our thoughts are beginning to be spread around the world, your world, and accepted as the truth, which they are.

Spacecraft in the past were not observed very often, but nevertheless there were stories around that abductions had occurred, and so mankind was frightened, naturally most people avoided spacecraft if they were sighted, in case they were abducted. Nowadays people are mainly delighted when they see a UFO, and feel that perhaps all of us are benevolent towards you, which we are. Those beings who abducted people in the past are no more, and banned from the planet, and only those who are friendly towards humanity are in the area. You know we have been assisting mankind over the centuries, both to you on Earth and to those on other planets in a similar situation to yourselves, on the third dimension, who are ready to move up onto that higher dimension of existence to which you are progressing. We hope that over the years you will accept our help and be ready to help others on your planet when the time comes for those changes to occur upon the Earth, which are inevitable.

All of you who read these words are more than ready to accept the truth, and ready to move upwards with your expansion of consciousness, and accept everything that will occur in future days. You and your families will be protected, and the coming changes will be gradual. You are in safe havens where you exist at present, and we hope that anything that happens will be mild. In the future, the changes that occur throughout the Earth will be quite dramatic, but as you know, you will already have ascended to that higher dimension and be able to see what is happening with open eyes, through your capabilities of accessing other dimensions. You will be able to help both yourselves and all those around you to be protected at all times.

Our spacecraft are still patrolling the skies above your Earth, and we access information that is coming in from our planet, and from members of the Ashtar Command, who join with us in this work. We are ready at a moment's notice to pass on knowledge to you, and others like you throughout the Earth and those other planets that we are assisting. Always remember that you will be the vanguard for accessing the fourth and fifth dimensions, we are from a higher dimension and we can tell you anything that you wish to know in this respect. From the sixth dimension we have been travelling over the centuries, through time and space, and we are aware of your trepidation at times. I know that you may think that when you pass into a higher dimension, you will be passing into spirit, but this is not the case.

You will be accessing a dimension that mankind has not known before, and will be capable of doing so much more to help others, as a result, because although they too in the future will be on that dimension, you will be capable of being on both the third and the fifth at one and the same time, and as a result, the time that you have on Earth will be completely different for you on the fifth dimension. As has been told you before, on these higher dimensions we are out of time, and therefore you will be able to do much in a few seconds on that higher dimension, whilst you exist on the third, so, although what may be occurring on the fifth dimension may seem like hours to you, it will only be seconds in Earth time. Therefore, you will be able to use that time to good purpose, if necessary, to help both yourselves and others before they too are on that higher dimension.

When the time comes, you will understand what I am trying to tell you, and know that you will be perfectly safe in your dealings with a higher dimension, and be able to move instantaneously from one place to another, which may be miles away, in the blinking of an eye, and without any means of transport, apart from thought. Miracles will happen, seeming miracles to you, but to us just normal life, because we can move through thought in space, as well as with our ships, so that if we wish to visit another craft ourselves without moving our spaceship, we can be within that other craft in seconds. It may seem impossible to you, with your finite minds, but I am sure that as your minds are open to the realities that exist on another plane of existence, you will be able to accept many facts that perhaps others would not be able to, with their three dimensional minds and limited acceptance of their possible capabilities in the future. You have much to look forward to, and your lives will be changed completely once you have moved into that higher dimension, and you will be able to see and speak to us very easily. Once you can see us, it will be much simpler, and you will recognise others and us as beings of light and with benevolence towards you.

When you expand your consciousness, and realise what you will be capable of, your minds will expand, and take in the fact that in the future you can use thought to transmit your thoughts to others, as I am doing to the channel at present, who is accepting my thoughts quite easily. You too will be able to speak to us telepathically, and your minds will be able to take in our thoughts and those of other beings. Your minds will become much more powerful, and will be used to great advantage during your future life. As we mentioned previously, through thought you can create many things, including food and articles that you might need for the future. It takes some time and practice before this can be achieved, of course, but once you have that accessed knowledge, your lives will change irrevocably. There will be no need for you to visit shops and stores, and other places where you purchase products. You will be able to create these for the life you will be living in the future, and it will be much simpler for you, and the manufacturing of goods will come to an end. You may need produce, such as natural foods, but in the main, you will be able to produce these also in future days through thought, so that once you have achieved this, you will be able to do many things through your minds that at present you have to do physically.

In time, your bodies will become more amorphous and less physical, due to your change in diet, and to the changes that will occur around you, therefore, your muscles will not be so necessary to do physical work. You will find that your minds will become more powerful, and you can use your thoughts for the good of others, which at present you are doing, using them for healing, both physically and absent healing for people who are distant from you. This capability will become much more evident in the future, and your minds will be used for so much more than at present. The mind can be a very powerful tool, but must be used for good always, as we do, and always have done for the good of all.

In time, all the earth dwellers will realise that what is required of them is just an acceptance that they should be at peace with one another, and that there should be no more violence and hunger for power in future days. It will take a little time, but once these changes occur, those who are still living on the Earth will be ready, and happy to accept this as the norm, and your New Age, your Golden Age will begin. You will see many beings from other planets who will be coming in friendship and accord, and you too will be able to visit other planets if you wish, the choice is yours. My brothers and I give you our blessing, to you all this day. God bless, Caristal.

CHANNELLED COMMUNICATIONS FROM SIRIUS, ARCTURUS, PLEIADES, & BETELGEUSE

SECTION FOUR

BETELGEUSE

CHANNELLED COMMUNICATIONS FROM BETELGEUSE
Book Four

CONTENTS	**Page**
Section 1 – Hvan	133
Section 2 – Hvan	136
Section 3 – Hvan	139
Section 4 – Hvan	143
Section 5 – Hvan	146
Section 6 – Hvan	149
Section 7 – Hvan	153
Section 8 – Hvan	157
Section 9 – Hvan	160
Section 10 – Hvan	164
Section 11 – Hvan	167
Section 12 – Hvan	171
WHAT IS CHANNELLING?	175

Channelled by Beryl Charnley

CHANNELLED COMMUNICATIONS FROM BETEGEUSE
HVAN-1

This is Hvan. Thank you for your greeting, I am so pleased to be able to communicate with you for the first time. We have spoken briefly before, but I am now ready to give you my thoughts, to dictate them for your teachings. It is difficult to decide on what subject I should speak to begin with. You are aware that I am from Betelgeuse, and that there are few of us who have been able to communicate over the years, so I am pleased that I was able to make contact with you earlier this year.

At times we feel that there is no change in the thoughts of humanity on planet Earth, but it is being revealed to us that gradually, there is an alteration in the consciousness of a certain group, including those of you who read these words. What is necessary is a dramatic rise in consciousness throughout the people of your world, in order to appreciate what is about to occur when you rise onto the higher dimensions. It may come as a shock to some who are unawakened, but I am sure that more will become aware and be ready to receive new ideas from you. Already there have been many programmes on your television screens, which are revealing this new awakening, a new interest in strange realities, the paranormal as it is called, but strangely enough, many of you have already experienced these ideas, and were ready to be aware of your spirituality much earlier as a result.

Our species have been evolved over the millennia, to be able to travel from one planet to another, and be able to contact the beings on various planets surrounding our area. We have been voyaging further afield, as time progressed, and therefore we have been ready to accept our responsibilities, in order to help others like yourselves, who are on the verge of discovery that the Earth is changing and has been doing for some time. There have been new energies pouring down onto your planet since the harmonic convergence, but so many are completely unaware of this. We have been watching and hoping you would be ready when the changes come.

Over the last century, several planets have been altered in their dimension, rising higher onto a level with ourselves, and we have been one of the many groups of beings who have been ready to help at the time. It is strange that you are not aware of any of us, you cannot see us and yet some can receive our thoughts. This is better than nothing, and we hope in time you will be able to see us face to face, so to speak, and therefore will find it much easier to be in communication. As more of you reach that level of consciousness, we will be able to communicate more freely with the people of the Earth.

We have craft of varying sizes to travel through space, and although some of our vehicles have been seen periodically, we are usually invisible to the eyes of mankind. We are present in the space around your planet, and have large craft to which smaller craft can go, and they are more like bases, almost like satellites, but not quite as large as you would consider a satellite to be, if you compare it with your moon. However, the craft that I am on is a very small one that may look like a little circular light to those on Earth. We have the capability of moving at great speeds, and we can move fast towards one another, and in that way we are able to move extremely freely in the space around your planet.

It may be that people have seen these very small vehicles, which may have confused those on your planet, thinking that perhaps it would be impossible to travel far in these, but you would be surprised at the distances involved, because we have our base ship to return to for supplies, rest and maintenance.

It is not a fuel that you would recognise, that powers our craft, but an antigravity method, rather like a magnetic impulse that propels our craft, the smaller ones, and we have been experimenting over the centuries with various means of transport. In time to come, your people who built craft and who experiment on various propulsion methods will come up with new ideas very soon. It is difficult for man to learn at the rate that we have learnt, but there will be help given, and changes will be made in powering your space vehicles in the future. There will be less danger involved, because in the past you always had to have large supplies of fuel on board the craft to propel it out of the gravity of the Earth, and there has been some loss of life, but changes will come in time.

It has been unfortunate that this has been so, but all who were involved were prepared to give their lives to enable the space programme to go forward. We have been travellers in time and space for a great length of time, and we appreciate that these dangers have always been there, and in the past, lives were lost from some of our ships. In the early days, they were in experimental form, but nowadays there is no danger, because of the experiences we have gained in the past.

Your astronauts have learnt much, and your discoveries of planets around you have been evolving over time, but this is nothing compared with what we know, because so many of your scientists and the thoughts of mankind have been blinkered by your finite minds. We are not being superior in talking in this way, because we realise that most of these scientific minds are only capable of logical, practical thought. They do not appreciate that beings can exist, which are invisible to your eyes, and beings of a different construction from your own can exist in locations that would be impossible for humanity, and the form in which they exist can appear strange to yourselves. It is only with imagination that you can realise that beings can live on planets that appear to be uninhabited. In the past they may have existed upon the surface, but over the centuries they have discovered they can exist more safely within the planet, and have constructed tunnels and vast living areas that would be impossible for man to realise, but nevertheless this is so.

As time progresses, I will be happy to tell you many things that you will no doubt be interested to learn about the beings on our planet, and those stars or planets in our area. You have an open mind, and those who read these words also, so I will be pleased to pass on my knowledge, and the knowledge of my brothers to you over these communications. For now I will close, and I hope that we will be in contact with one another very soon.

God bless and keep you all, Hvan. (Pronounced Hwaan).

CHANNELLED COMMUNICATIONS FROM BETEGEUSE HVAN-2

My greetings to you, this is Hvan. It is interesting to see how much attention is being given to U.F.O.'s, as you call them. Your civilisation is waking up to the reality of spacecraft and other beings. At last it seems that people are realising it is possible there may be life in the universe, and that humanity is not the only being existing at this time. It is strange to think that so many of us have existed over the millennia, perfectly aware of the Earth and its occupants, knowing that we are highly advanced, compared with you, but it has taken so long for mankind to recognise that there is a possibility that others exist. There seems to be no proof, according to your official reports, apart from the fact that spacecraft have been seen above the Earth since biblical times described in various ways, and yet it is obvious that this is what has been seen, and there have been efforts to describe the craft and the people who have emerged from it.

We have been watching the Earth over many centuries, and we recognise the fact that your people have had closed minds to this subject on the whole. There have always been some like yourselves who have open minds, and who recognise the fact that the truth is there, and that craft and their occupants have been travelling across space for millennia, either seen or unseen by humanity. We often cloak our craft by going onto a higher dimension, or using other means to make ourselves invisible to you, so that we cause no panic. Otherwise there could have been many problems in the past, and even now, because it is impossible to tell you the number of craft that encircle the Earth at times. Obviously we are aware that because we are on a higher dimension, and see others travelling around your planet, and other planets of course. We are not concentrating on the Earth alone, all are concentrating on other third dimensional planets, to help them also at this time.

As you are aware, it is a time of great change for your planet and those upon it, because of the raising of the vibrations onto the fourth and then the fifth dimensions. We have been on higher dimensions the whole of our lives, and we do not know what it is like to be third dimensional, but we recognise the fact that you are very vulnerable to danger. If you are third dimensional you cannot escape something that is travelling towards you at great speed, such as some vehicle, a giant wave, or something else that will destroy you.

Whereas, we can escape from any material danger of this kind, and lift onto an even higher dimension than we are at present. Most of us on planets similar to our own, are on the fifth and sixth dimensions, so we can avoid any problems of this kind. We are not so material, physical shall we say, and therefore the molecular structure is more widely spaced, and danger is not apparent to us. We cannot be destroyed in this way, as you are, those who are run over, or have some kind of drowning accident, as I have said with the giant wave, for instance. It is rather sad to see this happening throughout the world, because much life is destroyed in this way. We recognise the fact that your planet is highly populated, and perhaps this is one means of keeping the numbers down, apart from serious illness or even warfare.

There are times when there is more population than is ideal for a planet, and the result would be disastrous if your population were to increase even more, because in certain areas that are extremely densely populated, there would be famine or shortage of water. It would end up in a serious state, and as a result, I suppose there would be natural wastage, as there is with other living creatures. You see carnage all around you on the roads, where birds and small animals have been mown down by fast moving vehicles. This is just a simple example, an analogy, so you can compare this wastage with humanity. It seems rather strange to you perhaps, to be compared with birds and animals, but I am only suggesting that this must be a way of keeping down the numbers on your planet.

From time to time, obviously, disaster strikes in the way of earthquakes, or bombing via violent factions of your communities. We hope that this violence will eventually cease. So many have been working towards this end, and pouring light energies down towards your planet, which in time will take effect, particularly if those of you who are working with the light, like us, will join with us in this work. I know most of you are already doing work with light, sending it into the negative parts of your planet, and sending healing towards them and others whom you know need help. It would be wonderful if all of us could combine forces and work together. Perhaps this will be possible in the future, when more are able to communicate with us directly. We could arrange certain times of the day to unite in this work, and eventually this unity would have a more powerful effect than each one working singly or in small groups. It is always much more effective in larger numbers, as you know.

My companions and I on our craft are hoping in time you will see us face to face. This will happen once you have reached that higher vibratory level on the fifth dimension. I know that you are very keen for this to occur, and naturally we too hope we can help you in this, to reach upto our level of being. You find it hard to visualise how it will be, but do not worry, it will happen quite quickly when the time is right. Your minds must be attuned to the light. I know you practice meditation regularly, and reach upwards to bring down light through you, so you can join with that light and raise your consciousness. This is the only way you know, I realise you are hoping that one day each one of you will have achieved a new vibratory rate to bring yourselves onto that higher dimension. Gradually you will learn there are different methods besides bringing down the white and violet fire of light. You will find that gradually there will be a thinning of the barrier between our worlds, when sufficient light is brought through. It is difficult to describe, but your world is solid, or it seems so to you, being in three dimensions, but once the light penetrates you and the Earth beneath your feet, and both you and the Earth becomes more ethereal, then you will recognise the fact that all of us are one. We are truly beings of light, and you too are the same, but enclosed in physical forms more fully than ourselves, and it is this dissolving of the physical that is necessary for you to achieve, before you become fifth dimensional beings. Try to bring down a rainbow of light into your being. It is essential you are filled with light, and this is part of the plan for mankind, to bring him into an interdimensional state of being.

As you know, we move through the dimensions and through space at great speeds, and we are capable of many things that you would deem impossible. There is much for you to find out in the future, and it will all be of great interest, very important for your lives ahead. When you come into your own on that higher dimension, your Earth will have altered at the same time. Everything is changing as you know at present, but things will continue to speed up, and you will find you can achieve tasks at a much faster rate. In future, everything you do will be done in a fraction of the time it takes at present. There are things you will do, and will be able to create that you would not imagine. You will just think of something and it will be there, something you wish to create, a meal or shop item. Everything will change, so that your lives will seem miraculous in the future.

We from Betelgeuse have been advanced in this way for many thousands of years, and as a result, we find it difficult to describe how different our lives are from your own, but you will see when the time comes. We cannot explain everything to you, because it is not our way, and also you have the choice to change or not, but I think all of you who read these words will hope to gain these capabilities as soon as they can, and progress as the Earth progresses. In time you will join us and become members of the interdimensional brotherhood of the universe. Time will cease to exist, and you will realise how restricted your lives have been in the past, but then you have known no different, so you would not feel too inhibited as a result. There is much for you to look forward to in future days, and we hope to enlighten you further, as time progresses. I leave you with my blessings and good wishes to all, Hvan.

CHANNELLED COMMUNICATIONS FROM BETEGEUSE HVAN-3

Greetings to you, this is Hvan from Betelgeuse. I wish to talk about communication today. There are so many things you can consider when you think of this term. There is communication between one another, talking as you are at present, and communication between those who are apart, using the telephone, which you have in all your homes. There is also communication via the media, newspapers, radio, television, fax and mobile phones, all these are methods of communication on your planet, but very few of you use your mind to communicate as the channel is doing at present, receiving my thoughts as I think them towards her. This is how we communicate with one another; we do not need speech, or machines. Think how your lives would be if you had no instruments of the kind I mentioned at the beginning. You would feel lost and cut off, but it is perfectly possible to use thought as a medium for communication. This will be your main means of communication in the future.

The communication by means of channelling, as you call it, between perhaps beings of light and yourselves as physical beings of light, is another form of communication that will be prevalent amongst you in the future. You all have this latent ability built within you, but very few have discovered how to use it. Some of you, and those who read these words, have communication of some kind with their guide or God within, or other beings who are perhaps in communication with you. In the future it will be a normal manner of speaking with others, hearing their thoughts and passing your own thoughts to them, and this can be achieved in time. At present your capabilities are fairly low in this respect, you do not have the built in chakras in your bodies, to have strong and powerful signals given and received on the head. In the future, extra chakras will develop, and are doing so now, which will be utilised for this purpose, to form an antenna so you can receive and transmit using this antenna yourselves.

At present you have your third eye chakra and your crown chakra, but in future there will be several chakras added. There is one at the base of the skull, at the back, which may presently be latent. It has been there for some time, and is gradually being utilised by some of you now, and the one on the pineal gland will be utilised by the third eye instead of the crown chakra. The one on the pituitary, which is presently the third eye, will be extra, and externally there will be your crown chakra, and another chakra at the front above your head, and one behind and above it. All these chakras will combine together to form a type of antenna, to transmit and receive any information you can be given from other beings. We have had this type of communication for millennia, shall we say, and there are beings on other planets like our own who have this capability, and you in the past had this before

Atlantis was submerged under the ocean. It is something that sadly has been lacking ever since those days, when man was in contact with God on a permanent basis. It is perfectly possible for this to occur now, and will do in due course. All of you will develop these extra chakras in time, in order to communicate in future days.

Sadly, it is necessary for mankind to change his ways. All of you who read these words do not need to concern yourselves over this, but there are so many still who are of a negative disposition, and they have to be encouraged and sent light from above towards the areas where there are these violent factions. Fortunately for humanity, there is a sufficient number who are managing to raise your consciousness onto higher levels, and as a result, the Earth is moving upwards onto a higher level of being. You have helped this through bringing down the light and sending it into the Earth, as well as to others of humanity. It is important that you continue with this work, and I know you have every intention of doing so.

In fact, it is necessary for mankind to meditate and look within, and to try to develop this capability, and to learn to listen for that inner voice instead of reaching towards the noise that is prevalent around you, and not developing the spiritual side of his being.

It is difficult I know, to keep things in proportion when you are in a physical body, but realise that unless more people extend this capability, mankind will not as a whole, raise onto the fourth and fifth dimensions. We know you have every intention of continuing on the spiritual path, and those who are already set in this way will be safe and protected when the changes occur.

The Earth has gradually been moving towards the photon belt. This is something that I know some of you are aware is occurring, and this halo of photon energy is being projected increasingly closer towards the solar system. I was going to mention this last time, but it matters not, you are aware of it, and you know this will alter your lifestyles completely. You are aware that the electricity will fail for several days, and in future you will not need this power, so be prepared for three or four days of darkness and cold, when this time comes. The photon energy will alter everything in its path. It will cleanse and purify the atmosphere on and around the Earth, and you will be protected in a bubble of neutrality that has been prepared for you and the solar system, to dwell in the whole time you are in the photon belt.

All will be well, and once you emerge from the darkness at the edge of the belt into the light, you will realise you will have altered, and the Earth and everyone on it will be cleansed and empowered with the photon energy. Accept this for what it is, and is something you are destined to experience. I know that perhaps many will be worried about it, but this is unnecessary because the Cosmic Federation has conferred together in order to protect the Earth, and advice will be given to you at this time, and for some time to come. There will be beings from other worlds, other times and dimensions who will come to you and help counsel all of you through this time of change. We from Betelgeuse and the Siriuns, Pleiadeans and Arcturians are amongst those who are helping the Masters and the Angelic Hierarchy, all joining forces for the good of the whole to guide you through this time of change.

It is difficult for any of us to know exactly when this will occur. So much depends on humanity, and so much depends on the speed at which the Earth is moving. I know you are always moving in space, and all planets must do, but inexorably there is a movement towards this belt that is coming into your vicinity. When this occurs there will be these days of darkness, but once you have got over that time, you will find there will be improvements in so many ways, that it is something to really look forward to, and you will find you can do many things and all receive messages from beings of light once you merge into the dawn of this new age of photon energy. Master R has mentioned this to you also, I know, but there are always different sides to a story that must be told.

You have within you these chakras that will emerge and develop over time. There is also another one near the thymus gland that will prevent you from aging, and it will prevent you from many illnesses that man is heir to. As you are aware, the thymus gland is large within babies, and gradually dwindles as the child grows, and it is a gland that was present in the days of Atlantis, and always stayed the same size. Illnesses that you have on Earth now, were unheard of then, and people did not age as quickly as they do now, but gradually this will alter, and in fact many of you who are already aging will find they will become more youthful after this experience of the photon energy. You will be surprised at what will occur at that time. You will find as I have said, your capabilities to communicate telepathically will suddenly increase, and you will be able to see beings that exist around you, but you cannot see at present. You will be really delighted and amazed at this new capability, your curiosity will develop and you will wonder who all these beings are.

Once you have discovered they have been there all the time, you will be quite surprised at how many there are even in your garden, that you have never seen before, including the little people, who will be delighted that you can see them from now on. We too have devic beings and little people on our planet, and it is a delight to communicate with them. Of course we have always seen them, and they have been gradually communicating with more and more beings on other planets, who have learnt to see them. Like yourselves, there are only certain people who are able to see them presently, and like you, these people on other planets are learning to see and communicate with them. They too have raised their vibratory rate onto higher dimensions, like us, to the fifth and sixth, at which level you will find that all the other sentient beings will be able to communicate once you learn that capability.

We are able to communicate with other spacecraft through the mind, if we use it powerfully enough. It is possible for us to hold quite long communications with others, both from our planet and from others who are travelling through space around the Earth at this time. All of us have one thing in common, and that is to serve God, and be of use to as many beings as possible who are in need at present. So, communication can be all powerful, and the mind utilised in this way can overcome any lack of equipment, such as the telephone, television or radio, the signals of which will be changed once this photon belt appears.

You will find you can overcome anything like this, using the mind in a positive way, and with the facilities you will have in the future to transmit and receive from others, you will not need anything but your own built in capabilities. So there is much to look forward to in the future, in finding everything that you have been told about, and discovering new methods of communication and transport. All is there for the taking, and we will help and guide you in whatever way we can.

God bless and keep you all, Hvan.

CHANNELLED COMMUNICATIONS FROM BETEGEUSE HVAN-4

Yes my friend, this is Hvan, and I am very happy to greet you once again. We have been encircling this area and waiting for you to begin your meditation. We have never described our form to you, nor have we spoken of our planet Betelgeuse, which is extremely large, compared with your small Earth, but your Earth is a beautiful silvery blue orb, which we look forward to visiting frequently. Our planet is extremely vast compared with your own, and we are large compared with you, most of you. We are taller, rather like those from Sirius, but we are not beings of great broad stature, although our light bodies extend widely, rather like your own, your auras as you call them, because all of you are beings of light like us, and you are quite large beings extending beyond your physical form. We have much knowledge stored away within our minds, and we wish to expound on this knowledge to a certain extent. It is a time for you to learn more, and although many of you may know what we try to tell you, be patient and know it is for the good of all that we speak.

I think you are now aware that most of humanity has come from the stars. At various times throughout the history of the Earth, there have been landings from many planets and stars over the millennia, and these have either established groups of beings upon your Earth, establishing civilisations that either have continued or fallen into disuse. Over this time so many civilisations have come and gone, from different stars to your Earth, to try to establish languages, religion and culture, as we have done so many centuries past, but all of this is just a ground structure, so you will realise that your civilisation here on Earth was not based on Earth originally. There have been indigenous people here in the past, but most of you have come from elsewhere in the universe, and we are all in some way united, so that we could be related to one another. It may take a stretch of the imagination to think this, but some of you could have come from our planet, as you have come from the Pleiades and Arcturus, and perhaps Venus or Orion, Sirius or Andromeda. There are so many stars, planets, and constellations that have provided human beings on your planet.

Some of us are in your type of form, but others have taken on that form to dwell comfortably on your planet in the past. Perhaps it is unbelievable to you that this could be so, but I think you are realising that all things are possible to those on higher dimensions who come down into your dimension, to live here for a short space of time. The time that has elapsed when civilisations have been established on the Earth is but a fraction of time in the lifespan of one who lives on the sixth dimension or higher, even the fifth, because once you have passed through that fourth and fifth dimension barrier, it means you will find there is no much transition as death for thousands of years. Once you have realised this, you will recognise the fact that some of these civilisations that have created pyramids, statues and giant buildings all over the world have lived but a fraction of their lives on the Earth, and have returned to the stars, perhaps because of some disaster that overcame them. They realised they would be better off on their home planet, and had taken off in their craft, because once you realise these groups of beings were immortal, so to speak, you will realise they had not been devastated, but literally just vanished from the face of the Earth.

Sometimes they crossed that interdimensional barrier and even the time barrier, so it is difficult to say exactly when they established their culture on the Earth. Without being too particular, you will recognise that if you open your minds still further and recognise that time meant nothing to them, and that in the end, once they had established a culture on the Earth, they could take off in their craft and leave a population that would continue with the work they had begun. Many legends have started as a result of this coming and going of beings from other worlds. Perhaps they have been considered as gods, because they appeared in the sky, and landed on a hilltop, somewhere that has made the local, primitive tribes think God was descending from the heavens, or a god of some kind with disciples, whereas it was only men in a spacecraft, beings from other planets who had taken on human form for that space of time. So many legends have half-truths hidden within them; therefore it is good to re-read many myths and legends, with the thought in mind that probably they had been coming in craft from other planets. These so called gods, who came, helped, guided, and counselled for a while, and then disappeared.

What is necessary now is for all of you to keep an open mind and recognise the many truths that are being told you at present about the future of mankind. About how the changes will occur, and concentrate on helping to establish those new chakras that are rapidly growing, in order for you to be more telepathic in the future. Once you become aware of this, and concentrate on raising your consciousness higher, you will use these higher chakras more often, practice makes perfect, as you say, you will find gradually you will ease into a new rapport with those you communicate with in the higher realms. It is very important that this practice is done once or twice daily, to use these chakras in conjunction with your third eye and crown chakra, because unless you utilise this new faculty that is developing, it will not take effect now, and now is the time for you to create a strong channel between you and those who are trying to speak to you, your guides or other beings who normally communicate with you.

You will find this will give you more confidence for the future, when you will be using your telepathic powers to the full, because once the communication systems such as radio and television break down for some time to come, you will need this to connect with others who are at a distance from you. It will all take place quite easily once you have passed through that photon belt, and become truly fully conscious human beings, who can utilise those telepathic powers and all the other powers you will receive as a result of moving onto a higher vibration. We will be here to help you before the time, and afterwards to guide many people who otherwise would not know what is occurring. You will be helping those with whom you are normally in contact, and you will come to the fore, once these changes start occurring. Many will turn to you, if you reassure them beforehand, and try to explain how things will be altered in the future, for the better in so many ways.

It is a wonderful time for you to be incarnating upon Earth, and you will find all the things that have been promised, such as a new life, new world will appear before you eyes once the few dark days have passed, and you are truly within the photon belt. You will be lighter, exhilarant, and filled with energy, photon energy as well as your own energy. Everything will seem new to you, and you will come alive with that power that is there, latent within you, waiting to spring forth for that new day. Once it dawns, you will have everything in abundance, nothing will be held back from you, and everything that you would possibly need will be there to hand. We realise you are very restricted at present, compared with us, and although this is just the way you have always known, and never realised there were restrictions in your lives, the future is something that you can look forward to, and you will be as you truly are, great beings of light who are ready to help one another, and send forth love.

It is love that is the guiding force that helps us to help you, and all beings throughout the universe. All of us who are on higher dimensions are filled with love for you, and wish you well. We will speak again. God bless and keep you all, Hvan.

CHANNELLED COMMUNICATIONS FROM BETEGEUSE HVAN-5

Yes it is I, Hvan who greets you and all others of like mind. I am pleased we can speak once again, and talk of many things. Your chakra system is still expanding, and in time, all of you will be able to be in telepathic communication with other beings besides your guides and those who normally communicate. With these new telepathic capabilities you will gradually find you will be able to send communications to one another. As you know, once the photon belt has passed into your vicinity, you will have these powers, but it is good to try to use them to the full before that time, and to experiment with telepathy between one another. Some of you have a greater ability than others, but all of you with practice will find this power will steadily increase, and so you can attempt to contact one another before the time of the change. Obviously, I know it is something that you will have to plan ahead for at certain times. I believe this is already done within groups, and has sometimes been successful. In time, with practice, all of you will have this ability, and will be able to send communications and receive them in due course.

To begin with, it is advisable just to keep it simple, and try to visualise an object or a short message for each of you, to attempt to transmit and receive. What is necessary is to gain confidence in this, and with that confidence you will be able to achieve it much quicker than you would if you were idly thinking of something. It must be done with positivity, and the feeling you will achieve a result. It will be good for you to have this as extra interest, and to link with one another in this way at certain times. Obviously you have to have full consent of those concerned, otherwise there would be no point, and it would have to be at a designated time. Try it and see how you get on, and perhaps next time I speak to you, you will have achieved some good results. It may be quite amusing, and you may have some discussion on this over the intervening time. It is something that will engender interest between you, and will be better than negative subjects such as much of the news, and programmes that are rather horrific on the television. Do not attempt to watch horror programmes or violence. I am sure you know this already, but it would be far better to occupy yourselves in any free time to do this work, rather than idly look at newspapers or television that is often a negative influence.

I have said before, negativity begets negativity, and it is necessary to have all the positive thought that you can in the world at this time. Always use your thoughts positively, and with love, and then if you pass on this message to all with who you come in contact, the love and positive thought will spread, and gradually mankind will take on a new aspect. I do not mean that those who read these words are negative, not at all; it is just that if you can counter negative thoughts and deeds upon the Earth, you will be doing a service, because there is much negativity at present. Gradually the light will take effect, and that Christ light that you bring down each day will spread into all these dark corners of the Earth. We have been using light all our lives to good effect, it is something we have lived with constantly, and have never known anything else. We have always used the Christ light and our own light to be in service to God, and all living beings within the universe.

Most of us on the higher dimensions are benevolent, and we attempt to help other beings from planets that are like yours, on a slightly lower dimension, but always we keep in mind that it is necessary to have a positive outlook. There are beings who have descended on the Earth or close to the Earth in past years, and beamed up some of your Earth people to experiment upon them. All this is now finished with, and I think some of the programmes on television are misleading, because they make out that this abduction of mankind in twos and threes is still occurring, and it is not. This has been banned, and those who have done this in the past cannot now continue with this rather horrible method of contacting Earth dwellers, and I would wish all of you to dismiss these past experiences that people have had, from you minds. Always dwell on the positive, and know that any craft who are in your area are all benevolent towards mankind, and they are all like us, only here to help.

As we become used to one another, we recognise the fact that all of you who are working with the light over these past few years, are attempting to learn as much as you possibly can about us and other beings within the universe. Also, you are mindful of your own limitations, and are hopeful that within a short space of time, you will have accomplished the task of rising onto the fourth and then the fifth dimension. Through your dedication and discipline of meditation, you are achieving much, and we are pleased to say that many of you will pass on to the higher dimension before the photon belt appears. Therefore, you will be able to pass onto the higher dimension, the fifth, and then the sixth, within a short space of time. Once you have achieved the fourth, the fifth is far easier to negotiate. The transition from the third to the fourth is difficult. When you are meditating and communicating with us, your consciousness is on that higher level, your superconscious shall we say, and therefore you will find in time the rest of you will follow!

We are aware that you are on various levels of being when you meditate, and we appreciate that all of you who read these words, are learning and improving constantly. There is so much for you to learn, new aspects of your future life, and the capabilities you will have once that change has come about. I know all of you are attempting to read books on various subjects allied to this, and in time you will learn all of us are alike, in the respect that those who are joining with us in the work with the Angelic Hierarchy and the Masters, are all working to one end, service and counselling to all beings, and help in any way.

We are aware that you have all been sending light and love towards those upon the constellation of Lyra, and we have been helping in this respect for some time. They have exceeded their capabilities in many ways. Their technological achievement has been great, but the love aspect is necessary now, and I know you have been sending love and will do so for some time to come. It may be strange to you perhaps, that it is necessary for an evolved civilisation to have to ask for help from you, as well as us, but your planet is one on which the inhabitants were given free will, and therefore those of you who are working with God, love and light, have within you a great reservoir of that love. Now that you have opened your heart chakras to give and receive unconditional love, you have the capability of helping these beings who do not have this ability to love. It is good that you can help them at this time, because this will give you confidence to know you have reached a level where you can participate in our work within the federation of the galaxy. In sending forth your love to other beings on a planet that longs for this, you are joining with the Universal Mind or Cosmic Consciousness, in which we have our being. You too, while meditating, are part of that, although you have not yet achieved that higher level yet, but it is gradually increasing.

Over the next years you will become aware of much change, and you will find that all of you will feel that new telepathic ability growing within you. Concentrate on practicing your telepathic powers on one another. I do not mean you should eavesdrop on one another's thoughts, it is a matter of transmitting and receiving simple things, and this will help you in the future. Once you have realised we are all part of the whole, and we are trying to expand your knowledge each time we speak to you, you will realise it is not essential to buy endless reading material. It is practice that is more important. It is good to read around subjects to a certain extent, but practical learning, such as I have suggested, is equally important, and then you will be able to extend your capabilities over a wide range. Try this with one another, projecting thought, and you will find that very soon you will be able to receive those thoughts from each other quite a distance, and with improving accuracy. It will be amusing for you, and also help you for future days. I will leave you with that thought. It is a simple exercise for you to try, and one that we feel sure will help. God bless and keep you all, Hvan.

CHANNELLED COMMUNICATIONS FROM BETEGEUSE HVAN-6

Yes, this is Hvan, and I give you my greetings and love this day. I hope that gradually we can build up a power between us. It is good you realise that it is necessary to raise your consciousness onto the superconscious level, so we may communicate with ease. My dimension, as I have said before is much higher and therefore it is more difficult for me to reach down to your mundane level. By that I mean your everyday thinking in your consciousness, but if you raise higher, then I can speak to you more easily through your mind. I hope in time that others will be able to reach me, and I can communicate with more. Some humans can be taken over, shall I say, in a trance, and as a result their minds are completely blanked out, and our thoughts can more readily be absorbed, but this is a different method of communication, and I know this is not your way. It is more difficult as a result for us to interpenetrate our thoughts into your minds. I know it is difficult for you to link with me at times. I am speaking to you on a different level.

We hope that eventually we can counsel you, all of you, as to what will occur when the photon belt comes nearer to the Earth. At that time, much help will be required, and I know that all of you who are aware of this happening, will be able to describe what is occurring to those who are completely unaware of it, to your families, friends, and anyone with whom you come in contact. It is important that a warning is given to all, if possible, so that people can be prepared when the time comes, and the light gradually fades from the face of the Earth. It will be a time of great fear and panic otherwise, so it is important this is broadcast to as many countries and peoples of your Earth as is possible. It may be that your television programmes can be taken over for a few minutes, to forecast what is going to occur at the time. This will need to be done throughout the whole world, but it is possible for this to happen, and then there will be less panic, perhaps.

I know you are aware there will be very little disaster, at least on the scale you were expecting. It will be negligible, because in the past many of you have thought there will be catastrophe on a tremendous scale when the changes occur, but there is now a critical mass of people who have raised their consciousness onto a sufficiently high level throughout the world, which has tilted the balance to a more positive vein, and as a result, there will be less disaster throughout the whole of your globe. I am not saying there will not be some destruction, because with the photon energy it cleanses and purifies the whole of your world when it passes over it, and the whole of the solar system will be affected in some way. However, the protective bubble in which the solar system will be contained and enveloped will make a tremendous difference. This has been arranged, and is gradually occurring as time progresses. Those who are concerned with the solar system are building up the bubble of protection powerfully, those of us who work together, cooperating in this work. As you know, many of the Hierarchy are working together with us, and we look up to the Angelic Hierarchy and the Masters. We are all concerned with protecting everyone, and every being that lives in the solar system. You have no idea how many beings are concerned in this. It is like a vast army that goes forth through space, working to help you through this time.

I mentioned in my last communication that perhaps you might practice telepathy with one another, and I feel more and more that this is a very important thing to do, to work in cooperation with one another, and to try to extend your capabilities in this way, because just before the change occurs, you will need as much help as you can have, so that when the communications do break down, when the photon belt appears, you will find you can link with one another in this way. It is important that this can happen, so that you do not feel completely cut off from one another at that time.

Because of the darkness for those few days, you will have to stay in your own homes, of course. It would be impossible to gather people towards you then. That would have to be done before the photon belt covers the Earth, and as a result, it will be easier if you have this in mind, and things prepared beforehand. There is plenty of time yet, but it is well to be prepared in advance, so the telepathy practice will be interesting and beneficial as well for all of you. Try to arrange small groups who will cooperate, and you will find if you try to project a thought powerfully enough towards one another at a set time, that gradually your capability will improve, and you will be able to set each other more difficult tasks and messages, over time. Your confidence will increase as you practice, and it will be a good exercise for all of you to do on a regular basis if you can. It is a very important part of the learning process, and once the photon belt arrives, in that first few days, you will be ready to communicate with one another. After that it will be natural for you, you will have that natural ability because you will have passed into a higher dimension, once the light breaks and the dawn of that new age begins.

When that time comes, positivity will reign supreme, and negativity will be banished forever, because the whole Earth and everything upon it will be cleansed of negativity and violence, and the whole of your world will be a place of peace, and you will be true beings of light. You are already, of course, but your bodies will be revitalised, and they will become lighter and more amorphous as you move higher onto the fifth dimension. Everything will be new to you, and you will find new capabilities that at present you cannot imagine. We have abilities that we realise you are incapable of realising at present. Your minds will be clearer and less finite, and you will reach new heights of awareness. Once the photon belt edge has passed over you, and the light dawns brightly, you will be able to do all these things and more, like we can. Everything that has been said in the past about miracles, you will be able to do. Create and produce food in an instant, and move from one place to another in an instant, using your mind. The mind, as I have said before, is all-powerful. It is a tool to be used for good, and must always be used in a positive way, but once you have achieved this new vibratory rate; it will be even more powerful than before. It will be more powerful than it has ever been in the past, and you will find that you will be able to utilise many abilities for the benefit of others.

At present you use your minds to bring down light, and send out that light and healing to wherever it is required, but in the future, that power will have increased tremendously, and you will find that healing will take place instantaneously through using your hands and minds for the benefit of those you wish to help. This has been practiced by those of whom you are aware, like Jesus, Buddha, and present day Avatars, who can use this power because they vibrate on a higher level than you, and can access the fifth dimension.

I think you are already aware of this, and recognise the fact that they have had this ability, either in the past or in the present. You too will be as they, and you will be able to use this power for good. Never think of using it in a negative way to overpower others, that would be extremely sinful, and I am sure would never occur to any one of you, and those who would have used this power for evil will have been banished from the Earth for good.

Do not worry that violence will break out again, because new governments will have to be formed, and legislation occur to a certain extent. This will be taken care of, and there are spiritually aware advanced beings on the Earth who will help in this work. It is gradually being organised now, so when the time comes, they will be ready to accept that honour and responsibility in the future. Certain people in each country are being gradually groomed for this future role, and they will accept this responsibility and be ready to help when the time of the change occurs. You will realise it is important there should be people ready to accept this, and be prepared when the time comes. Obviously those who have only wished for power in greed will be overcome, and this will be taken care of at the time. There are many things that will change in the future, but it is all for the better, and we and others who work with us will be ready to help you when the time comes.

The people of our planet have been in this situation in the past, many thousands of years ago, but we assure you that everything on our planet is now peaceful, and our life is one where there is much to live for. You will realise this when the time comes, and be grateful in the future for this communication with beings from other planets who have experienced what is occurring to you at present, and are aware of the doubts in your minds. Be assured that all will be well, and you and your families will be protected and cared for. We give you our love and blessings, and wish you well. God bless, Hvan.

CHANNELLED COMMUNICATIONS FROM BETEGEUSE HVAN-7

This is Hvan, and I am happy to greet you this day. I know that on this planet at this time, many people are turning inwards and reaching up their consciousness to higher levels each day. The more they meditate, the higher they can receive the energies and communications that are pouring down towards the planet at this time from so many sources. Once a prayer is said, protection is given and more of you are able to channel these communications towards themselves. As time progresses, this will happen, and all of you will be able to receive whoever wishes to speak to you. It may be your guide, an archangel, or your higher self, or even Sananda. It may be one of the Masters, or like this channel is receiving me, a being from space. Everything will be possible to all of you who truly have faith in your own spirituality, because that power is latent within each one of you, and only needs awakening. All of you in time will be able to receive our thoughts and messages of hope and good will towards all of you.

It has been a time of great change, and this change is accelerating. You must be aware of this, and recognise this new awakening is spreading throughout the world. It is what is called the Second Coming, although many of you imagined that the Second Coming would be Christ appearing on the Earth once more, to give hope, comfort and counsel. It is, however, coming from within you, and instead of having the physical presence of Christ upon Earth, you have within each one of you that guidance and comfort that is really far better. It means that eventually everyone upon the Earth will be capable of receiving all these communications that are being given at this time, and will continue until everyone is able to receive. I know perhaps there may be disappointment with some, because they will not see the physical presence of Christ upon the Earth, but it would be impossible for him to visit each one of you, and present his physical presence before you.

I know perhaps television coverage would change things from the time your Jesus Christ lived upon the Earth, and there were only a handful of people, shall we say, compared with the whole world, who actually saw and heard him. Even so, his message lives on, and has spread and stayed with all of you who believe in him, because the Holy Bible was written around his life, and the lives of his disciples, and spoke about the miracles performed in those days. That is the New Testament of course, the Old Testament is not strictly accurate in so many ways, but told of many occurrences at that time. It spoke of a wrathful God, which is not true of course, because the God whom you worship is the God who was present from the beginning of time, and who is worshipped by so many. It is true there is a God of all, the Source of all being, which has existed since the beginning of time, but time of course is different from the time of Earth, to time with us, which is virtually non-existent, however it is too involved to try to interpret it to you, when you live on a third dimensional planet.

It is extremely hard for you to accept the fact that time goes on forever, like an endless stream, and has done since the beginning when God came into the universe. The original universe that has increasingly expanded to many universes over the many millennia since the word of God came, 'That which is and always shall be.' We too believe, and we know that the great being that came into being, shall we say, has created so much, but we realise that your minds are very finite, and cannot always accept everything as it truly is. Suffice to say, that time began from the time that being came into operation, but your time is more set than ours. Time can expand, and is elastic, and it can go forwards or backwards. We live in a different dimension from your own, and we travel through time and space, so it truly is completely different for us than it is for you. Gradually, as things change for you, it will become clearer to you, as you rise up into that higher vibratory rate, and you will recognise what it is I am trying to say, when the time comes.

Your minds are becoming more powerful, and as time progresses, you will recognise the fact that through your mind power you will be able to create both food and things. By things, I mean material objects, food itself of course is material, but we are thinking of mostly produce, and the material objects will be more solid. Their molecular structure is more compact, and these objects will be variable, whatever you wish to create, and truly have the faith that you can do it, so it will be. Sometimes simple, such as a chair or table, but at other times, it may be a small mechanical object. Time will tell, and you will discover how powerful the mind can be, once you are on that higher dimension. It is something that is beyond your thinking at present, but it is something to look forward to for the future, because everything will change for the better, and although you may still have doubts about this, wondering how different your lives will be, do not worry about this. It will evolve gradually, by that I mean it will occur within the near future, but you have time to think about it and prepare for it, it is not going to happen overnight.

Everything that is going to occur, you will be given due warning about. You will be helped in many ways by beings of light, be they from other star systems like myself, or the Masters and Angelic Hierarchy, who are working with us, as you know, or rather we are working with them, shall we say. It is difficult for you to accept that all of us are combining together. You always felt we were separate from one another, a different life stream, but this is not important, so long as we genuinely wish to work together for the good of all. That is at the back of everything, and our reason for living is truly one of service. We hope in time you will accept these facts as the truth. I know that some of you do, but there are those of you who feel this is a vision that will not happen, but have faith and know it will come to pass. There are warnings to be given to those who have not yet awakened, and I hope that before too long, you will be able to give this warning to as many people as you can.

I know some of you have been trying to spread the word, shall we say, but at times it is rather difficult to broach the subject, and drop that seed into their minds that changes are occurring, and to actually speak about these subjects. Fortunately now, there have been more programmes on the television on subjects such as the supernatural, UFO's and strange occurrences, which can be a lever for you to speak about these things as being natural. Many people still seem to shun these subjects, and would not dream of watching them, but perhaps in time you will be able to persuade them they are worth watching, and that there is truth within these programmes that is worth knowing about. I certainly hope you can manage to do this, because it is important, the changes are happening throughout the world, and will involve everyone, and they too need to be warned and awakened to this fact.

I, Hvan, am trying to communicate with a number of people upon your planet to spread the word, and to give wisdom to as many people as possible, so the handful of people that I communicate with is worldwide. Not all on this island of England, but in America, China and in Europe. One or two other places also, which I felt was important, so the word was spread right across the globe. It seems it is being accepted that channelling is a normal occurrence, with certain people, because now it is realised many books have been written in this way. In more recent years, the number of books that have been channelled has grown tremendously, and therefore the spread of this type of spiritual knowledge has accelerated greatly over the last few years. It is important that this is so, and as I said previously, these books in time will not be necessary, because all of you will have this facility to be able to tune in to those in the higher realms on another dimension. You will realise once you have done so yourself, it is just like your guide speaking to you, or your higher self.

Some of you, perhaps, have not yet received word from your guides, but you will if you persist with your meditations daily. Twice daily is preferable, because you make faster progress that way, and will increase your confidence in the work.

It is time for me to leave you now, but I give you this thought that you should practice attempting to send messages or symbols to one another. I have mentioned this before, and I feel it is important to repeat this. Try to visualise something, however simple, and send it to either someone else in your home, or have a set time for sending these thoughts to others who are interested in this work, because it is important to develop this telepathic capability that you all have. It is important to spread telepathy horizontally, to one another, on the physical world, as well as receiving telepathic messages from us in the higher realms. Remember to try to do this whenever you can with one another, sending and receiving at a set time. This will help you for future days. I give you God's blessing this day, and leave you now, Hvan.

CHANNELLED COMMUNICATIONS FROM BETEGEUSE HVAN-8

Greetings to you, it is good to speak again. You are all making headway in your bridging into the world of light. I am delighted this is so, because mankind had a large step to take, which is gradually being made by so many over several years. We have been watching the progress of all, and we know the energies that have been pouring down to you from above, have been taking effect, and although many are unaware of this, there is a large proportion of mankind that has gradually come into higher consciousness, expanding that consciousness onto a higher level. While you are meditating, you are raised onto that higher plane with your higher self, that part of you which has lived so many incarnations, and is fully experienced in many ways. You may not realise this, but you are very large beings of light, and I know that you are presently within your physical body, whilst you are physically involved, but whilst meditating and communicating with beings on another plane of consciousness you are larger, you are higher than you are at present in the physical.

It is perhaps difficult to put into words, but that part of you which is communicating is on that other dimension, the fourth, attempting to reach onto our level of being. Many of us find it difficult to come down into the heavier density of the third dimension, but as you reach higher towards us, it makes it easier for us to communicate on that higher level that you have raised upon. Many spacecraft, star ships and other vehicles are circling the Earth, becoming more apparent at times to humanity. We have been present for many decades now, we from Betelgeuse, but now we are communicating with many parts of the world at one and the same time, because many of our ships are present, and we are able to make ourselves known to you. Although we have come through time and space to visit you, we appreciate the difficulty you have in relating your experiences to others who are completely unaware of their ability to communicate with their guides or other beings of light. So many are completely unawakened, and living in the physical and material life without knowing the scope they have.

Fortunately for mankind, there are sufficient numbers now, to warrant the passing into that higher dimension being less disastrous than was first conceived. It was always hoped this would occur, and that more of you are able to pass on your knowledge to those now still unawakened. All that will happen, will be changes in the Earth's structure, I say all, but I know you are doubtful that things will remain comfortable for you. If it happens that the changes will affect you rather drastically, then it would be necessary to raise you in our star ships temporarily, only for a short space of time, but we do not foresee this. We feel that at that stage you will have reached the point when you can pass into the fourth dimension, before the fifth, so you are not affected. It is difficult for you to think of this, because you imagine your bodies will be injured in some way, but this will not be the case. You are to be protected in every way, and if there is any danger at all, you will be warned of this in plenty of time.

The photon belt approaches, but as it is in another dimension, the scientists are completely unaware of it. It will not reach the Earth for some time. The time, as mentioned before, is elastic, and it is always very difficult to predict exactly when something will occur. You know you have been told this so many times, you perhaps think it is an excuse, so that we can wriggle out of something we have prophesied! But this is not so, do not think we are attempting to do this! We hope you will have the faith to appreciate that time is man made, and that the forces in the cosmos are so gigantic that the Earth herself is but a pinprick in that universe of which you are a part. So it is rather difficult for you to appreciate the vastness of the scale of everything that is occurring in the cosmos. Suffice to say, that warnings will be given before anything occurs that may affect you, and in that time you will be able to gather together everything you will need in the way of provisions, and whatever will affect you, and your families can be prepared in that time. What is necessary is practice in raising the consciousness, practice in telepathy and practice in having the true faith that all will be well.

We have much in store for you. I am speaking not as royalty, as you might think, but as a group. We work together, as you know, with many beings who are attempting to help the Earth and those who live on it at this time, so we are speaking generally. We are helping in so many ways, that your minds could not accept, but we know you believe in us, and that you will have the true faith to know what we are doing, and have been doing for some time, is taking effect, and is helping the Earth at this time of change. So the transition should be smooth for you, as it was with us so long ago. Others helped us at that time, and we appreciated it, and once we were through that time of transition, we decided we too would like to help other planets at their time of change. So, many of us who were trained in space travelling, as you call it, volunteered to do this work as part of the Plan. We try to work in service to God, and all the beings of light who serve Him, we too believe in Him, and everything that was made by Him, and all beings who were created by Him and serve Him too. So we join with them in this large-scale plan, and work for the good of all. Rather like the Angelic Hierarchy, we too are here to serve, and do what we can to carry out the Plan that was formed so long ago.

Everything is ordered. There are many laws to which we adhere, and you would not conceive of the number of spacecraft, star ships and beings who are involved in the work. It is not just the Earth, there are several other planets and stars who are being helped through this time of transition also. Not necessarily in the solar system, but within the Milky Way, which is tremendous, and I know you can only see a part of it from the Earth, if you know where to look, because astronomy is quite a vast subject, and there is so much to learn. Many of you have no idea where certain stars and planets are, and we understand this, because you have your own affairs to contend with and other interests. When you see a beautiful starlit night, you recognise the fact you know very little about each star, and exactly where it is in the heavens at different times of the year. Because you appreciate there is movement in the heavens, and the Earth of course, so there are star plans that you are aware of, and which you can check periodically if you are sufficiently interested. I know some of you do try to keep track of certain stars and constellations, from time to time, but when it is cloudy for many nights, you are unable to see any stars, and perhaps feel cut off from us, but that is not so. The clouds are merely wisps, and the stars are always in the heavens, always there as points of light, and hope for the future.

    We are your hope for the future, and you know we can be relied upon, and you can communicate with us whenever you wish, if you will raise your consciousness sufficiently, and think clearly towards us, we will be aware of you and your wish to communicate, and your light will shine forth towards us. All you have to do is to try to shut off any other thoughts you may have in your mind, any other sounds that may be around you. Cloak yourselves with light, and we will be there to communicate and hear whatever it is you wish to ask. Perhaps some of you may have questions to ask? We will be very happy to answer them if you wish to ask. Always remember we are here to help you, and your questions can be answered as far as we can with the knowledge we have.

    Do not worry about the future. Remember there is a great deal of change ahead of you, but it is all for the better, and the Earth will be cleansed from all pollution. The Earth will become fair, green and beautiful to behold. You will find the water that may be scarce for a while when the changes come, will be cleansed and purified, and after a short space of time it will all be clear and drinkable when the edge of the photon belt has passed, and it is surrounding the Earth and the whole solar system. A bubble of protection will surround everything in the solar system, but nevertheless that cleansing will make all your surroundings clear and safe for normal life. Everything that lives on the Earth will be protected as far as possible. We hope perhaps you may have questions for the future, but in the meantime we leave you with God's blessing and peace to all, Hvan.

CHANNELLED COMMUNICATIONS FROM BETEGEUSE HVAN-9

Greetings my friend, it is Hvan who speaks, as you expected, and I wish you all well. I know you have continued with your practice of meditation, expanding your consciousness, and sometimes I know you feel you are not progressing very fast, but believe me you are all doing very well. All is well, and we are pleased with your progress. It does take time to rise onto that higher vibratory level, and in the process of change, your bodies, minds and consciousness change in many subtle ways, of which you may be unaware.

Most of you who are ready for the change within the Earth are succeeding in all that you attempt to do, but I think the telepathy is still something that leaves a little to be desired! Maybe your practice has not been as often as it might have been. I know it is difficult to fit all these things into your busy lifestyle, and when on the third dimension you are busy, physically, it is not always possible to fit everything in, but it is only once or twice a week, and will be important for the future. As you know, all communications will end for some time when the Earth changes occur, and it will be a precious gift for you to have this telepathy. I know once you have reached that higher level it will be easier for you to communicate, but it is good to practice now, so you have that at your fingertips, so to speak, to communicate with one another while it is more difficult to travel, until you have learnt that mastery of teleportation. This will occur later, because until you reach the fifth dimension, it may be rather difficult.

I am presently considering what may be done in the more immediate future, for you to practice, apart from the telepathy, and is something that has to be considered. You have to think of how things will be when that time comes, and you are aware that electrical gadgets will be of no further use for the time being, and therefore, when you consider how many things depend on electricity in your present lifestyle, you will recognise the fact that you will have to do more through physical activity, instead of switching on a machine that will do the work for you.

In time, as we have said, you will only have to think of something happening and it will occur for you, rather like switching on the washing machine to do your washing, you will only have to put your clothes in a bowl of water with something to wash them, and you will find with practice they will be washed for you! It sounds amazing to you at present, and you might perhaps think that a good fairy will come along to do this work, which would be rather nice at present, but believe me, all things are possible once you have that power within you, that mind power that will be extremely strong once you have raised onto that higher vibratory level. You just have to have the faith that this will be so. We had to have faith when the transition came for us, and in time you recognise the fact that everything has been promised to you will come to pass.

This New Age for you is the time of mind power, it is something that you recognise has been occurring over recent times, and more people are able to use their minds to channel, communicate, healing and sending thoughts of love and gratitude to whoever has been helping you, which is to God or beings of light who have been pouring down energies upon the Earth for some time. You have all been using your minds much more than you used to, bringing down light, because all of you are light workers, and have been for some time. This power that has been generating within you and the Earth will be used to good effect in the future. The light which has been brought down from the realms of light has been utilised by you and many people are working in the same way that you are with the light, using it for cleansing, healing the Earth at this time, and those upon it who have been suffering in any way, including the animals. This light that you have used is something that is deficient in many star systems, including Lyra, Galea, Parthon and Zerros.

There are other stars that are in need of light throughout the cosmos that we are helping, and who are in great need of help at this time. The beings upon these stars have been missing the light of God and His love. It is unfortunate they have been devoid of this light and love for many years, but now Sananda and other beings of light have been visiting these stars, and helping to readjust this within the beings who are in great need. Some have already been helping in many ways, including those within the constellation of Lyra, you have been aware of this. You have been told it was necessary to send them light and love, and some of you have been projecting this, and trying to help where you could. If you can direct this light and love to the cosmos in general, having brought it down from the Source, you will find you work is of great help towards all these other stars who may be evolved in many ways technologically, but their spiritual side has sadly been neglected. Therefore, you are doing a good service in projecting this light and love towards them. Many of you have been doing this, and I hope these words will help to spread this great effort and necessity for these beings to as many others as possible.

This is a very important time for those upon Earth, and all of us who are attempting to link with you, because those of you who are aware of the light and have been using it have been attempting this link, and I know that through this your lives will be changed for the better, and the lives of those with whom you have been linking. In the future all these star systems and the Earth will find a brotherhood of light and love linking you and making you one. You are all a part of the whole, as we are, and although you have been upon the third dimension all your lives, and have been separate beings, you will find that once this transition occurs, you will feel a brotherhood with all the cosmos, because you are one. Most of you are from other parts of the cosmos, and have just been separated for the time you have been dwelling on Earth. There is that separation once you are born into that physical life of the third dimension, but it was necessary for you to come here to experience the lifestyle and to be a part of Earth's humanity.

All of you have had lives in which you have participated in temple worship, or have been beings who have come from other star systems, as I have said. All of you are experienced souls, evolved much higher than you might imagine. I am speaking to all of you who read these words, because if you were not reading these words, you would not be awakened beings. There are many whom you know who need to be awakened at this time, and I know you are doing your best to pass on your knowledge to those who are still on the verge of waking up to the fact they are spiritual beings of light, much larger than your physical selves. Your auras spread far beyond you, and all that is part of you, the light being which you are, reaching upto your higher self on the fourth dimension. I have said this before, and I know you are aware of this, but I am just reminding you of your capabilities that are there latent within you.

Now, perhaps there may be a few questions for me to answer before I leave you. I know you wished to ask one question, and that is, what is the difference between spacecraft and star ships. It may be that you are confused between the two terms. Spacecraft are those smaller vehicles, that circle the Earth close to the planet, and which many have seen, and sometimes they appear disc shaped. That is their normal shape, and can be any size from about forty feet to one hundred feet roughly, in diameter, but the star ships are very much larger than this, and usually do not descend low enough for Earthlings to see us. However, at times they have been seen, and we are usually in these larger ships, unless we are visiting to pass on communications, such as today, and we beam down from the smaller spacecraft that is stationed above the house, normally unseen.

You also ask whether we can recognise one another's craft. Yes, all have a different construction. Each star or planet has their own style of craft, although sometimes they may look very similar to you, if you do see them. We are aware telepathically in any case, of whether the craft is our own or from another star system, but normally one can tell, because of the slight difference in construction. Also, you have asked that if the disaster is too much to protect you when the changes do come, whether it is all planned, the method of raising you from the Earth. Do not worry about details, all is taken care of, and you will be given full protection should it be necessary. There will be beings from different stars hovering around the Earth in their spacecraft ready to help, if it is at all necessary, but we hope the critical mass of humanity who have expanded their consciousness sufficiently, will be bringing down enough light to counteract any catastrophe that might occur on the Earth at the time of change. So we do not foresee too much devastation at that time. We know you have faith in us, and in God and all the light beings, Angelic Beings and Masters who have been pouring down energies upon the Earth, and that when the time occurs, all will be well. In the meantime, I leave you with my blessing.

God speed, Hvan.

CHANNELLED COMMUNICATIONS FROM BETEGEUSE HVAN-10

My greetings to you all this day, it is Hvan here. I am very happy to speak to you once more, and to communicate anything that may be of help to you at this time. Sometimes you may think the Earth will never recover, there is violence in many parts of the planet, and suffering of many peoples, but believe me, this will become worse before it improves, I am afraid. It has to come to a head before mankind will recognise that something must be done, something radical before good can come out of it. The light will prevail, it always does, but it takes time before this New Age appears on the Earth. Many of you have been helping to bring down the light, and to try to encourage others to join with you. I know all of you who read these words have been working to this end, and you occasionally feel there is very little progress when you look at the news on television, but there will be progress within a fairly short space of Earth time.

Gradually the build up of energies and light have been generating power within the Earth and all of you. That power is strengthening, and as time progresses, this power of light will erupt and eradicate the negativity. I am not saying that it will erupt in violence, but the light will overcome the evil that exists at present. There are various ways in which this will occur, and in many places, key points within the Earth where this power is gradually building to a force that will suddenly take effect. There are places throughout the Earth of which you know not, but these power points have within them certain elements that have been built in, since before humanity was recognised upon the Earth.

Many beings of light existed before man came here, and they worked on the Earth, using their power and wisdom to build in these key points that are beneath the surface of the Earth, and exist upon higher dimensions. They have been there since long before man, and it will only take a little extra power to activate them, and to bring about a wonderful change upon the Earth. It is something that is arcane, and which we have been aware of, and the beings of light who created it, set aside these places of power for future times. All light beings who have been helping the Earth throughout the ages have been waiting for the time when this new change will come about. Working to the end that mankind will eventually learn this secret, and take his part in the plan that was organised for him aeons ago.

All will be well when the time comes, and you will find that at the approach of the photon belt, this new change will come about. We have known about this capability upon the Earth for a long time, and of course those beings of light, the Archangels and Masters have known long before we did, because they were some of the beings who set out this plan, this power plan, shall we call it, upon the Earth, and these key points will be activated just before the photon belt passes over the Earth. So, as you are aware that changes will occur at that time, there is also this plan that was executed so long ago, which will come into force, and counteract many things that might have happened when the photon belt passes over the Earth. There is power that will be generated, and can give light in the darkness. Think on these things, and know there is always protection for you all. This plan was set into operation, and it will be taking place at that time the photon belt comes.

We from Betelgeuse have been watching and overseeing your progress over many centuries, and we recognise there is a core of good within humanity, which we have, and we are happy that all of you have that benign attitude towards others, that love towards those who are less fortunate than yourselves. Your love spreads out towards the cosmos, to send light to other stars that at this time do not have God's light upon them. We have been helping, along with the Archangels and Sananda, and other beings of light, to bring about that change within these stars. To bring light to them, and gradually this is taking effect, and protecting those who are vulnerable.

This has been a time of great activity. You may have been aware of lights in the sky, as though pulsating, and some of you wondered about these, whether they were spaceships in the distance, and yet they appeared to stay in one place for so long, that you obviously thought it must be a star. Then sometimes it seemed as though there had been movement, and this radiating light was coming from a completely different direction.

It can be bewildering, unless you have powerful telescopes to pick out these particular points of light, believe me, they have been spacecraft. There have been many who have been attempting to send light towards you, to send their love towards you, and the only way it was possible for you to know, was to show this pulsating light, emanating from the craft. Of course, there are countless stars in the sky, particularly in the autumn when they are so clear on a frosty night, but there have been many appearances that certainly were not really stars.

You have looked out many nights, and occasionally when you have been watching these stars, as you thought, there has been a projection of love towards you, and you have felt you were being protected and watched over. This is true, because many of us in our spaceships have been sending out unconditional love towards the Earth now and again, because we felt it was necessary, and we wished to help in whatever way we could. Always remember many craft are unseen above you, and they too project light and love towards you, so never feel you are alone, or that you will be vulnerable at any time, because much protection surrounds you.

There will always be people who will look upon these thoughts as being ridiculous, because they do not have an open mind. They cannot think of other beings living on stars, which are virtually unseen from Earth, or in universes beyond the universe that you are aware of, their minds are very finite. It is only when you recognise the fact there can be many stars and planets inhabited by beings that are not humanoid, and not necessarily made of fluids, but altogether different in their structure from anything that you could imagine. Nevertheless, even if you could imagine it, many of them are in a different dimension, and they are also on a different time scale from the Earth. The Earth is restricted in many ways, as you are discovering, but gradually, as time progresses, you are escaping from those restrictions, and you will become fourth and fifth dimensional, so you will be able to see these craft and the beings who visit and watch over the Earth with kindly thoughts towards you.

The light that has been generating within you and the Earth will gradually take effect, and that light will overcome the darkness. We have been working to that end, and all of us from Betelgeuse have been attempting to radiate light into your homes, so that you who read these words will gradually soak up that light into your very beings, and we hope it will assist you in your ascension onto that higher level of being. We have found that gradually we have been ascending onto a higher plane of existence, as the years have gone by. Naturally all beings progress and evolve, and as we evolve, we raise onto still higher dimensions.

Space and time mean nothing once you have reached that level, and you will find that your lives will be less restricted in so many ways. You have found that as you take more time over your meditations, you feel that time slips by very quickly, and you lose all sense of Earth time when you rise to that higher consciousness. So it is in daily life, once you are on the higher dimension, because time is non-existent, and it is only on the Earth that your time is relevant. It is necessary for your way of life, but once these changes come about, you will not need that lifestyle to which you are accustomed. Do not fear that there will be so much radical change that you will feel lost. Everything is planned. There will be no chaos, we assure you, so just accept this, and go with the flow, and have faith that the future is going to be a wonderful one for all of you. Your families are all protected, so never fear. We will speak again, but until then, God Bless, Hvan.

CHANNELLED COMMUNICATIONS FROM BETEGEUSE HVAN-11

My greetings and love to you this day, it is Hvan speaking. I know it is important for us to link together in this way, for humanity to keep a communication link with all of us who are living in the cosmos at this time, or as many as possible, because that link is essential for mankind's future. He will then know he is not alone, particularly when the changes come to pass, in a more obvious way. I do not wish to be alarmist in any way, and I hope that when the transition occurs, it will be smooth. We are all here to support and help you, and we just wish you to know that mankind has arrived at a historic point in his evolution, at this time. You have been aware of many alterations in the climate, and in man's outlook towards the Earth that he lives upon. It is important this is so, because the Earth is also in the transition stage, and ready to ascend like mankind. So this stage is all set for an important leap into the unknown. Do not fear; it is not like stepping from a spacecraft onto the moon, or another planet at this point! It is just a leap in consciousness, and a change of dimension.

You have been aware of the fourth dimension, touching upon it when you are meditating, and gradually rising into it, as you have experienced that alteration in consciousness over the years, that you have been practicing meditation. Now you are more aware of what you are about, mankind will assume the fourth dimension, and is virtually there now. It is just another stage on the path to his true spirituality, and you are ready to take this step forward now. All of you who read these words have been working towards this end, and in time it will occur. It is a rather nebulous thing for you at present, particularly for those who are not able to see clairvoyantly. I know you have to have faith, and the confidence to go ahead without fear; it is just like stepping into another room. It is just another transition stage for you.

As you think on these things, picture yourself lying in bed, attempting to get to sleep. Sometimes you just lie down and close your eyes and there you are, you have passed into sleep without thinking, this is the same. Other times you spend quite some time tossing and turning until you finally merge into a dreamless sleep. This is another example of how it will be passing into another dimension, sometimes the more you struggle with it, the harder it is. Just allow it to occur, go with the flow, and you will realise it has happened without any change of thought, word or deed, it has just occurred, you will be there without realising.

Perhaps this sounds involved, but it is not. Just wait for it to happen, and continue with your meditation work, and gradually you will realise you have achieved that stage, and subsequently following on very fast behind will be the transition to the fifth dimension. Then the change will be much more apparent, and you will be able to see many beings, and be aware of so much more, once you have achieved that stage.

Working in the dark is a difficult thing, and this is what most of you have been doing, something that is just a state of mind and you feel there is nothing to show for it, you cannot talk about it to many of your friends who are not on this spiritual path. So although it is a very important part of your life, it is kept in the dark, nevertheless, it will come forth into the light, as soon as you achieve that fifth dimensional state, and things will begin to happen very swiftly then. People will then seem rather nebulous to you, and you will see other beings more clearly. Everything will change, but it will be for the better, and once you have reached this state, you will be able to help those friends who will necessarily have to join you on that higher level, because the Earth will have passed into that higher dimension, and they must keep up with you.

It is important that you 'keep your head when all about you are losing theirs and blaming it on you' as Rudyard Kipling wrote while on your Earth many years ago, and many of his words were extremely true and worth remembering. That 'If' poem is an important one to remember at times of change or doubt, it keeps you on an even keel like a ship, to avoid it sinking, you must remain with all hands on deck! Many of your sayings are extremely apt for this time. Keep on an even keel, and remember that what is occurring is very important.

It is a stage of man's evolution that has not happened before, apart from the first beings who lived on the Earth, who were very amorphous, and in touch with God constantly. They evolved into man as he is now, but you are all changing and returning to that original state. So it is a most momentous time, and you must realise how your reactions towards others should be gentle and understanding. All of you who read these words are aware, and you will be able to pass on the knowledge that you have, to those who are not aware.

We on Betelgeuse understand what is occurring, because this transition occurred on our planet centuries past. We have been travelling through time and space towards the Earth over a long time now, attempting to help, but we who live on a very much larger planet than yourselves, have a unity of mind with you, and although we do not resemble you greatly, we have a body which is built similarly, though very much larger than yours. Because of the different gravity, we have to adjust much more fully than those on a smaller scale than you, like the Arcturians. We find it rather difficult to assume the proportions that you have, and as a result, it takes a little time for us to adjust when communicating with those of you who can hear our thoughts.

I, Hvan, am perhaps eight feet tall, like most of our inhabitants, and we are larger in every way than you. We have limbs like you, and our hands, though large, are quite dextrous. This is necessary as we use our hands like you do, and also radiate light from them towards others.

It may seem strange that we produce light from our hands, but the light emerges in rays, and is used to control as well as emit light to energise other beings. This light from within our bodies is something that is used for many purposes. It can create energy for others, and for uses like how you would use electricity by switching it on in your homes. We have an energy radiation that we can use to activate energy in products, e.g. some food or drink you wish to warm. This can be energised, either to warm it or give more nourishment to it.

That is the only way I can explain it to you, because until you can see this radiation from us, you may not envisage it well. It is a different concept for you, and for now I can only say this is a purpose of ours, and we use our hands to generate that light towards others, and also to machines. Instead of pressing buttons as you do, we point a finger at the machine and it will begin to work.

It is a different way of doing things, and a different way of life, but of course our lives are very dissimilar from yours, in many respects, though it is interesting to see another lifestyle on other planets and stars. You may have thought that humanity was the only type of being that had lived on other stars and planets before living here. I know your minds are gradually expanding to accept much more over these past years, and gradually you realise if you keep an open mind, there is no end to what you can learn about spirituality and the different pathways that other beings are set upon. The beings from other stars can have also lived on a different star to that which they presently belong.

You may think we have always lived on Betelgeuse, or the Arcturians have always lived on Arcturus, or the Pleiadeans have always lived in that star system, but we have, like yourselves, lived in past incarnations on other stars. Maybe this is a new thought in your minds, and you will be surprised at this, perhaps, but it is the truth that all of us throughout the cosmos have been scattered around on different star systems in the past.

There is throughout infinity and time, a great change occurring, although change has occurred since the beginning of time. You are gradually discovering much more, and realise how limited your way of thinking had been in the past, but do not blame yourselves for this, because many are amazed at the truth, and this is what you are presently learning. Knocking on all doors, and waiting for them to open for you, and keep learning more. That is what life is all about, to learn, evolve, and try to experience as much as you can in a lifetime. When you realise how many dimensions there are, you can recognise we have gradually evolved from the third dimension ourselves, and through our incarnations, have learnt so much on other star systems as you have. Now that you are on a third dimensional planet, you are experience what is strange to you, and are gradually evolving to the level that you have been before, perhaps many times, but during this lifetime on Earth you have discovered a great deal. It is much more restricting for you, being in this physical body that is bound to the gravity of the Earth, even though your whole body is not seen, your spirituality, your aura extends beyond you towards your higher self on that other level of being.

You will continue to learn, and teach others in due course, just as we are attempting to teach and guide those who are ready to accept our thoughts. We are happy to do this work, serving all, and generate that knowledge that we are ready to pass on to those of you of like mind. You are our brothers and sisters, and you may begin to realise this is so, when you think that we have all been part of that cosmic brotherhood in the past and future. God bless you all, Hvan.

CHANNELLED COMMUNICATIONS FROM BETEGEUSE HVAN-12

My greetings to you, it is Hvan speaking. There are still things I have not spoken about to you, and this is our last communication. It is important for you to know; during the transition there will be changes in the climate of the Earth. This is something you are aware of, that you country will cease to be as cold as it is, the winter will hold no perils for you. The climate will be more temperate throughout the whole of your planet, so the extremely hot areas around your equator will cool and the whole Earth will be of a similar temperature. Naturally the north will possibly be a bit cooler than the equator, but in general you will need less heating in your homes. Although the changes will be something that has not occurred for millennia on Earth, many stars and planets are presently altering, and there is always change throughout the cosmos. There are always new stars manifesting throughout the many universes.

Always through change there is growth, and you will find you are capable of growing and expanding your consciousness very easily. You have recently found your consciousness has expanded already, and you have reached higher levels in your meditations. This is good, and will continue to improve as time progresses, and you gradually reach onto that new dimension more fully. You have been learning how it will be when you are upon that higher dimension. There are many books around that describe many entities who live on other stars, but it is not necessary to know about this. You will be told in time, and will eventually meet some of these beings who will visit and try to guide you in new ways.

All those who visit the Earth are now benevolent. There are none who will perform experiments on people, as was done in the past. It was done to understand humanity, but those who performed the experiments did not seem to be aware that those who lived upon your planet had their own lives to live, and were intelligent beings. It was done almost as though you were insects, or animals to experiment on, as they felt inclined to do so, but that is all finished with, and there will be nothing like that in the future. Those who may eventually visit your planet will be genuinely helpful. We hope to see you in the future, and naturally we will look out for those of you who have read these communications and other past communications from Sirius, Arcturus and the Pleiades, which this channel has brought through. Naturally, there will be visitations from other beings now and again, but that will be when you are accustomed to this, and not before. We do not wish to frighten anyone, because all of us look different from you in some way or another.

Most of you who read these words have seen programmes on the television such as Star Trek, which has accustomed most of humanity to the idea that there will be strange looking beings to yourselves, who dwell on other stars and planets, it has done a great deal to open people's minds to this awareness, which otherwise would have been lost to them. It is important that mankind is aware there are numerous beings of all kinds, who live on other planets and stars, and who have been aware of the Earth and its gradually occurring transition.

Besides the Earth, there are other planets and stars that are at this stage of evolvement, and you will find that after a period of time has elapsed, there will be travel to and from these planets and stars, from the Earth to them and visa versa, so all of you will become more interlinked. It may be that there will be important news given to you in time, and you will find this news will be concerned with space travel. Of course, this may not happen for several years, so don't expect the announcement on television in two weeks time! But nevertheless, it is a new possibility that will occur, because the travel will be much simpler, compared with past exploration with your present space ships.

You will find that once on a higher dimension, there will be so many changes that your life will be transformed, for the better of course. Space travel will be so much simpler without the rocket fuel, that is presently involved, and even travel through teleportation will occur once you are on the fifth dimension, and have become accustomed to the new outlook. Once teleportation has been achieved, you can visit many places throughout your planet with great ease, and will not need vehicles so much if you just plan to just pop over for a day or two somewhere. You can be there without any problems, and there will be transport of course, but that transport will be of a much simpler nature than your present planes. There will be great changes in this respect, but of course that is something for the future. At present, you are still living in a physical, three-dimensional world, and therefore you can realise that your minds are finite.

Once you have achieved that higher dimension, your minds will expand tremendously, to take in all this new knowledge and awareness of the limitless possibilities for the future. You will find that your capability of telepathy will improve, although some of you have practiced now and again, and this will be an advantage for you for the immediate future, later you will find that the mind will become extremely powerful, and your speech will be less necessary, because you will be able to send your thoughts quite long distances.

At present you can only be telepathic with one another in the same room, or experiment from the next room. In the future, telepathy will be used extensively, as it is on many planets at present. Many of us do not use speech as such, but in speaking through a channel of course, it is through thought or telepathy, so language is not required. The thought is there in the mind of the individual channelling, given them without any language barrier at all.

Just think of how it will be in the future, instead of your heavy automobiles and buses, you will be able to have your own little miniature space ship, which can travel just above the ground, so you will not need roads as such. You will be suspended above the road by several feet, probably, and you will be able to see exactly what is coming towards you, as a result, instead of going round corners with hedges or walls around you, as you do at present.

You will be able to skim over the countryside quite quickly, and instead of using roads, you will cross at the quickest point, so long as you don't bump into any dwelling houses on the way! It will be a different aspect altogether for you, you will find that you can travel individually, as you might say, as the crow flies, and so in future there will be no problem with tarmacing roads and putting up signals for traffic. Everything like that will go by the board, and you will have fewer restrictions in so many ways in your lives.

Your children and children's children will grow up in a new world, where there will be peace and a quality of life, which at present I feel is lacking in 'civilised' lives, shall we say. It is something that may have escaped your notice, because you have become accustomed to it, but there will be more time to stand and stare, and to examine nature and all its beauty. More time to be at leisure and enjoy life to the full in so many ways, which may show themselves to you in due course. Everything takes time to adjust, but I am sure the new life that stretches ahead of you is something you will find much more attractive as you think about it. You know you will have capabilities of creating food, as well as other products, and you will have less need to go to the shops, as a result. There will be no need to grow vegetables and fruit in your gardens, because you will be able to produce these at the drop of a hat, so to speak.

Everything you wish for in a simple way can be yours, so long as greed does not come into it. You cannot produce gold or silver, or something that is like a precious stone to sell, that will not be your way, I am sure it isn't at present, but all these things I mentioned in the last sentence will not have any value. It will be like a system of bartering, perhaps, because money will be valueless in the future. There will be different values, and this will have to be worked out, of course, by governments and those who will be in charge, in future days, but you will find there will be less legislation, and there will be no need for prisons, and all the complicated structure and hierarchy of the legal system. Things will be simple and straightforward, and you will find that crime will be non-existent. All this is something for the future, and I know it may seem strange that all this can be so, but it will be, and you will find that what I have said is the truth.

I have said that we have power in our fingertips, to radiate light, and to control many things. You too will have this capability, eventually, but until then, you can use your mind to develop it as best you can. It will all be mind power in the future, because the physical capabilities will not be so important, and the power you will use will be given to you from God. It is that divinity within you, the light that will be used for this power. It will generate within you, and as you live good lives, linked to the light source, then will that light source return that light and love to you to use for your own good, and for the benefit of all. Everything we are talking about is for the good, and we know that those who are violent upon your planet will be swept aside at the time of transition. All is well, and perhaps in time I will speak to you once more in the future, but for the meantime, God bless you all, Hvan.

WHAT IS CHANNELLING?

For anyone who has not so far heard of channelling, it normally occurs after the recipient has become accustomed to meditating regularly. He or she is used to listening to that still small voice within; not really a voice but thoughts that are dropped into the mind by their guide, or eventually, a higher being such as an angel, deva, or a master.

There is normally a signal such as slight pressure on the top of the head, which is what I experienced as a sign to take notice, and to still any random thoughts and listen within.

The ascended Masters are souls who have incarnated many times and overcome every difficulty experienced by mankind, and triumphed over all adversities that man is heir to. They have become true Masters of everything and only wish to help mankind in whatever way they can. They are members of the White Brotherhood, who exist mainly in spirit form, and gather in an area of the Himalayas and other remote areas around the world.

www.ingramcontent.com/pod-product-compliance
Lightning Source LLC
Chambersburg PA
CBHW061650040426
42446CB00010B/1665